# LIANG GUO
# DRAWINGS

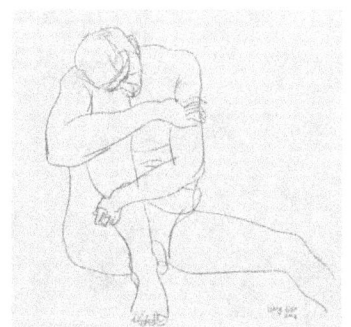

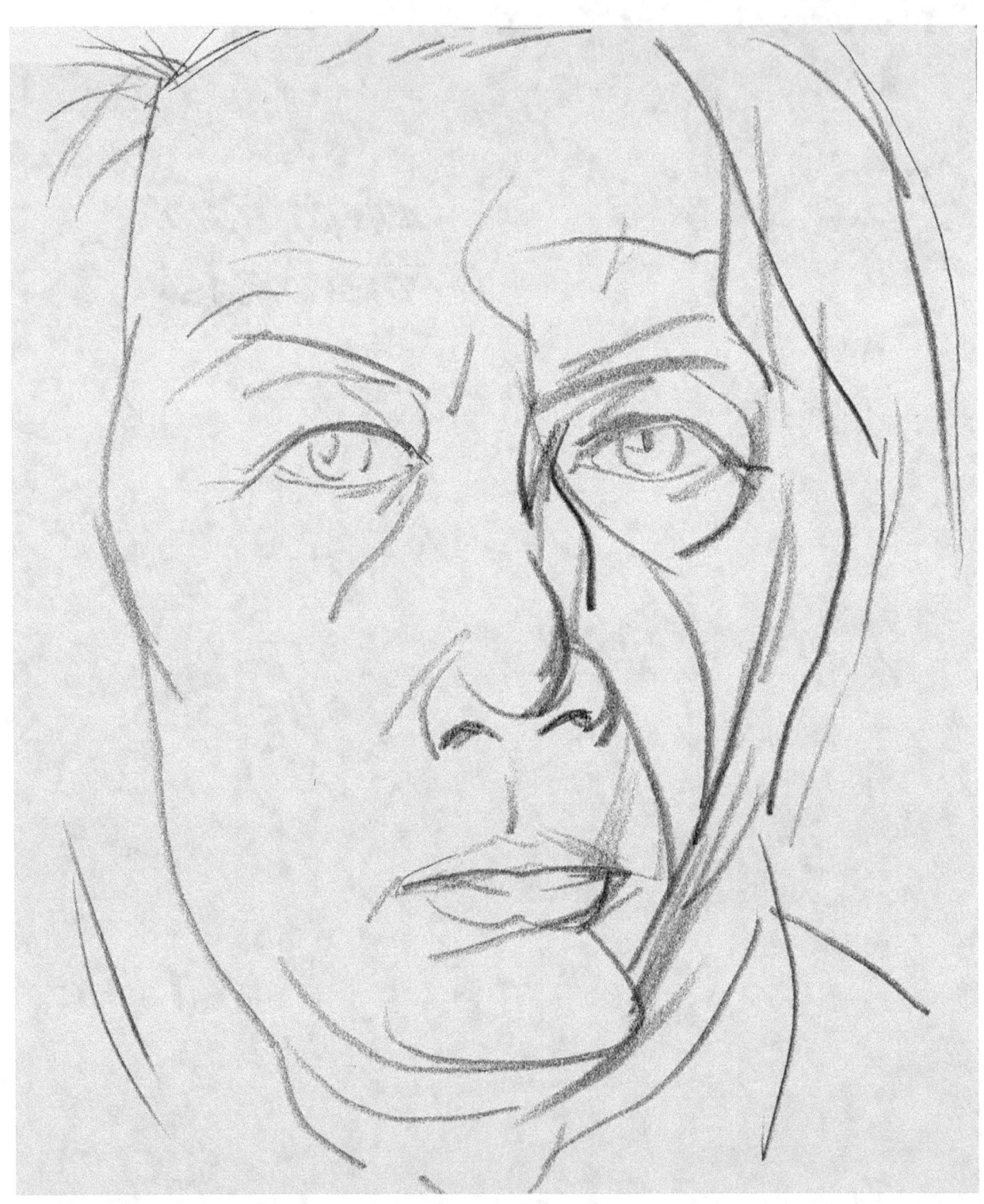

Self Portrait, 2012, Pencil

# LIANG GUO DRAWINGS

## 68 WORKS

SELECTED BY MING LU

Printed and bound in US

ISBN-13: 978-1477447444
ISBN-10: 147744744X

# Selector's Note

Liang Guo, a Boston-based contemporary artist, focuses on oil paintings as his daily work, and treats his drawings as his side-products. Actually, he has accumulated over 2,000 pieces of drawings in the past few years.

Liang Guo's drawings are all from live figures. No matter more or less time he spent on each individual drawing, no matter more or fewer lines he drew, no matter much or little shade he used, he said that he did them more than just by his hands and his eyes. Art is a bridge connecting the artist's soul to his viewers'. In this booklet, 68 drawings from Liang Guo's accumulation are selected to dedicate to the people who like drawings and use them as a mean of communication with the artist.

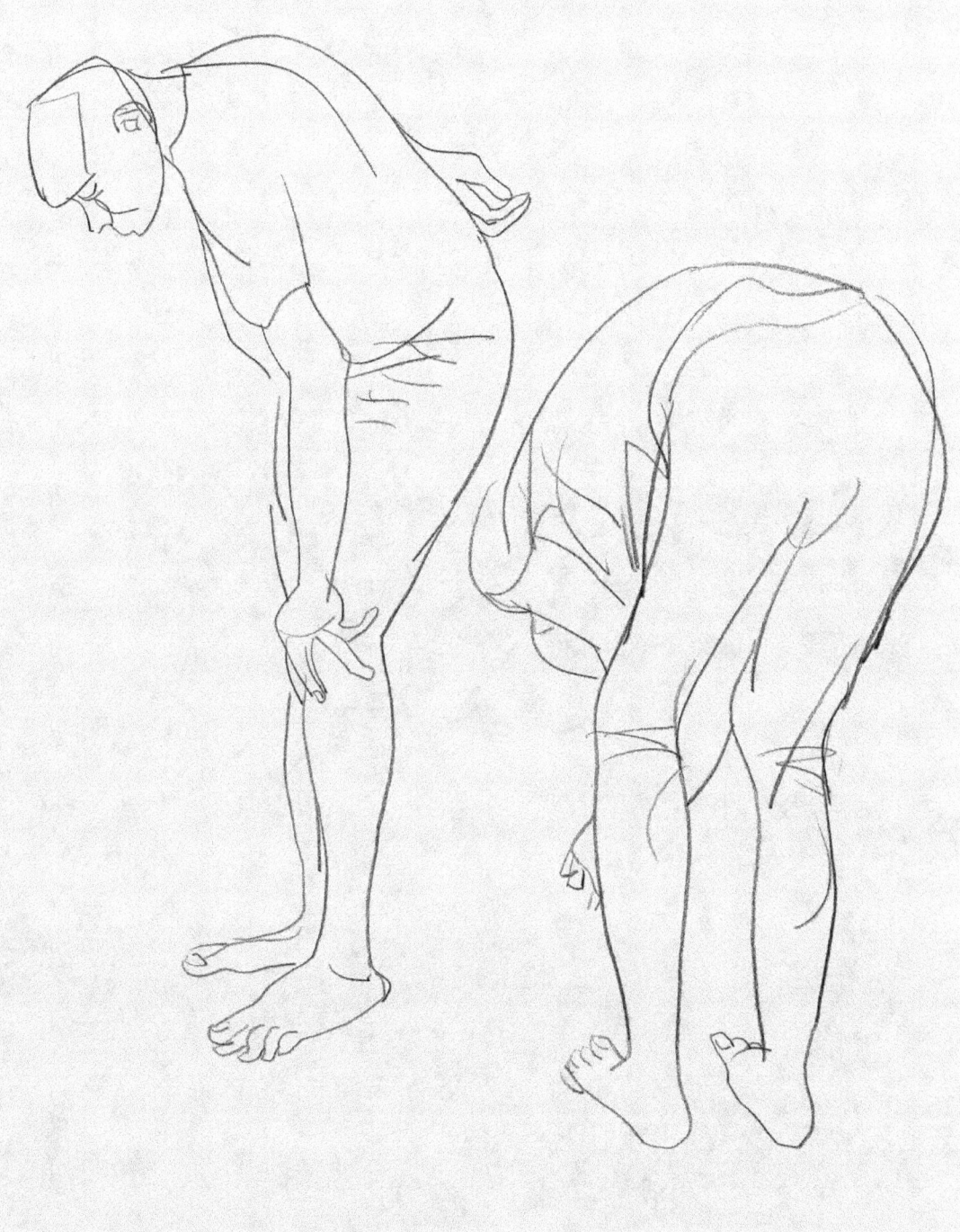

Liangouo
8—06

1    Searching, 2006, Pencil

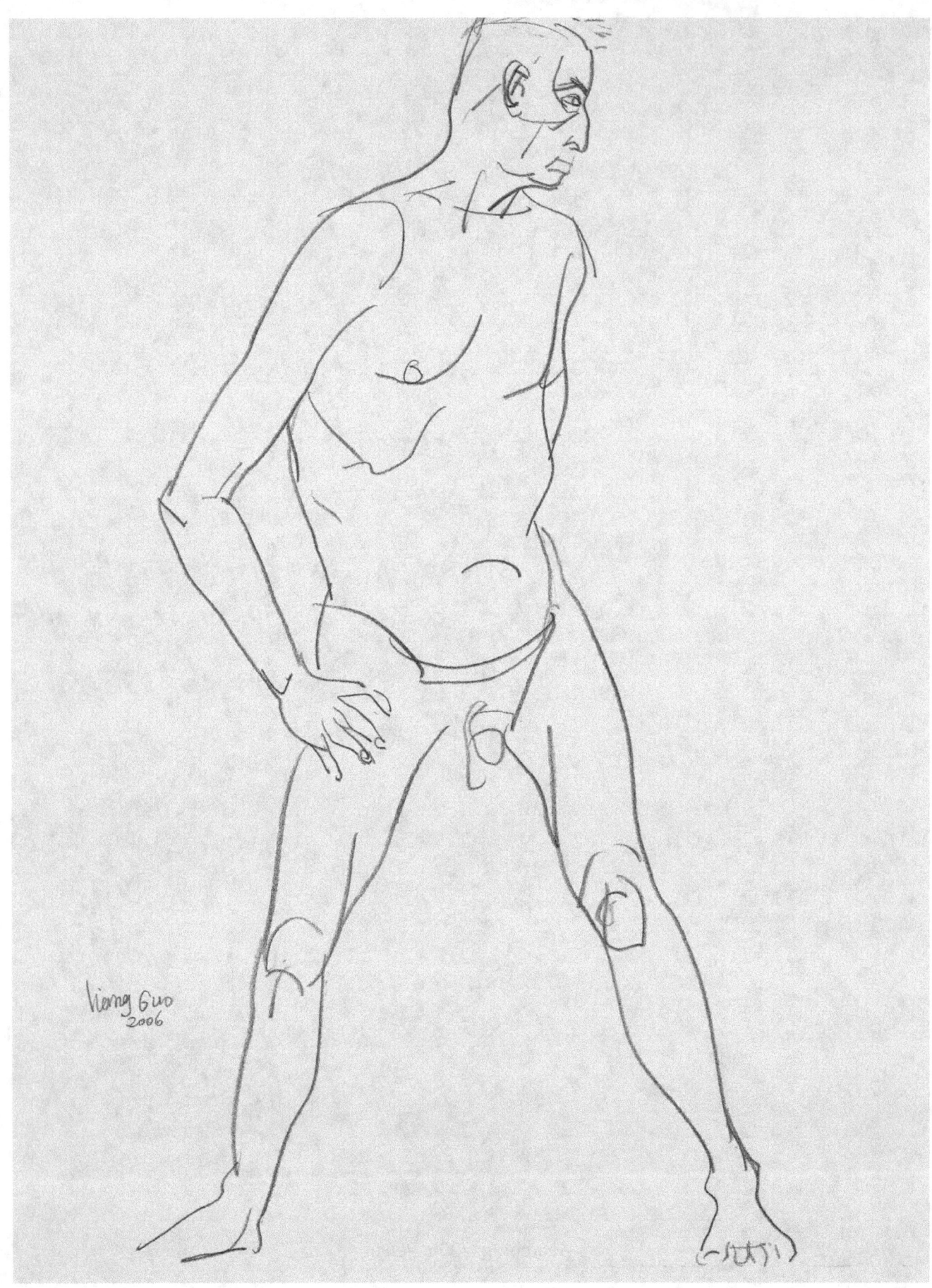

2    First pose, 2006, Pencil

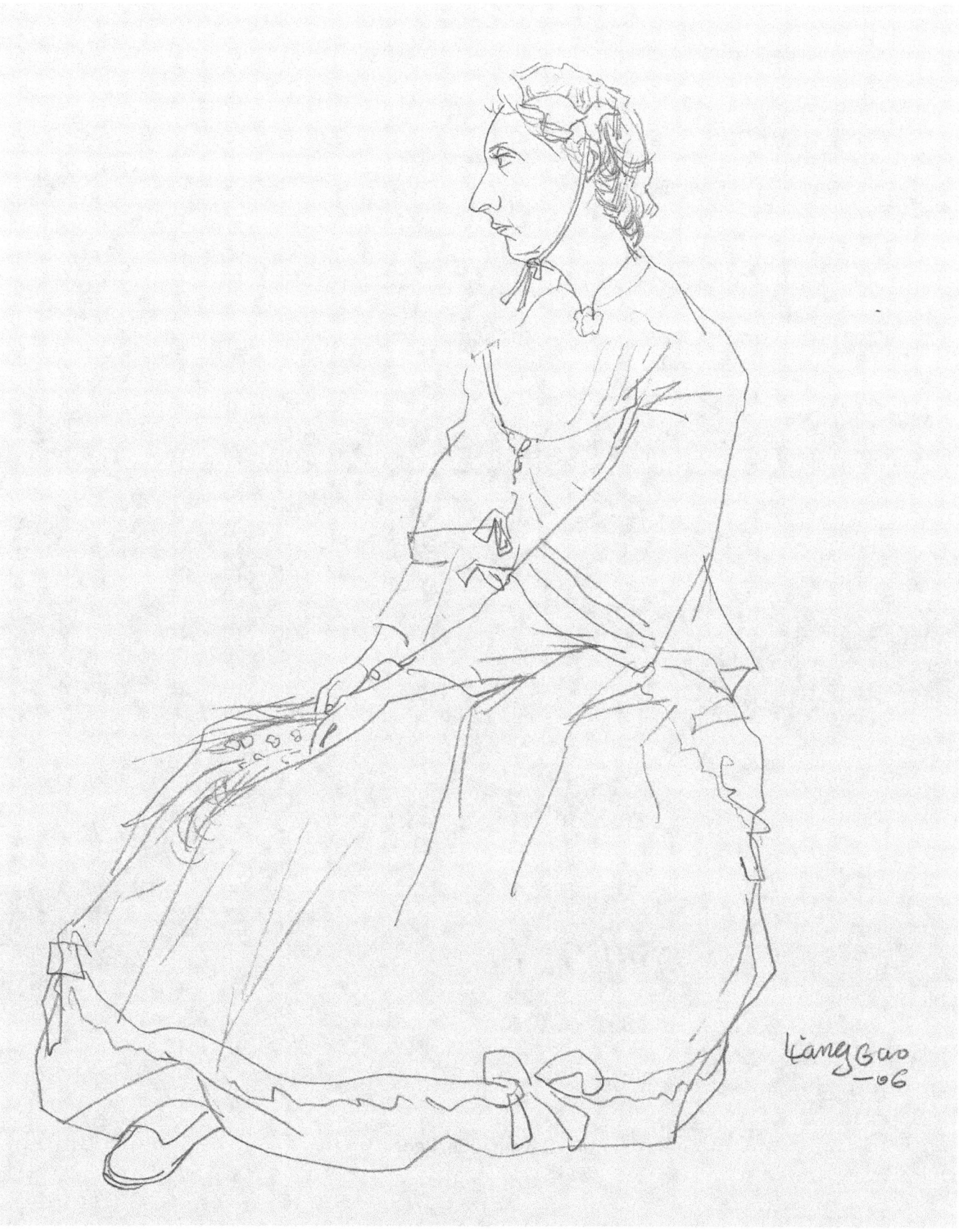

3    At that old time, 2006, Pencil

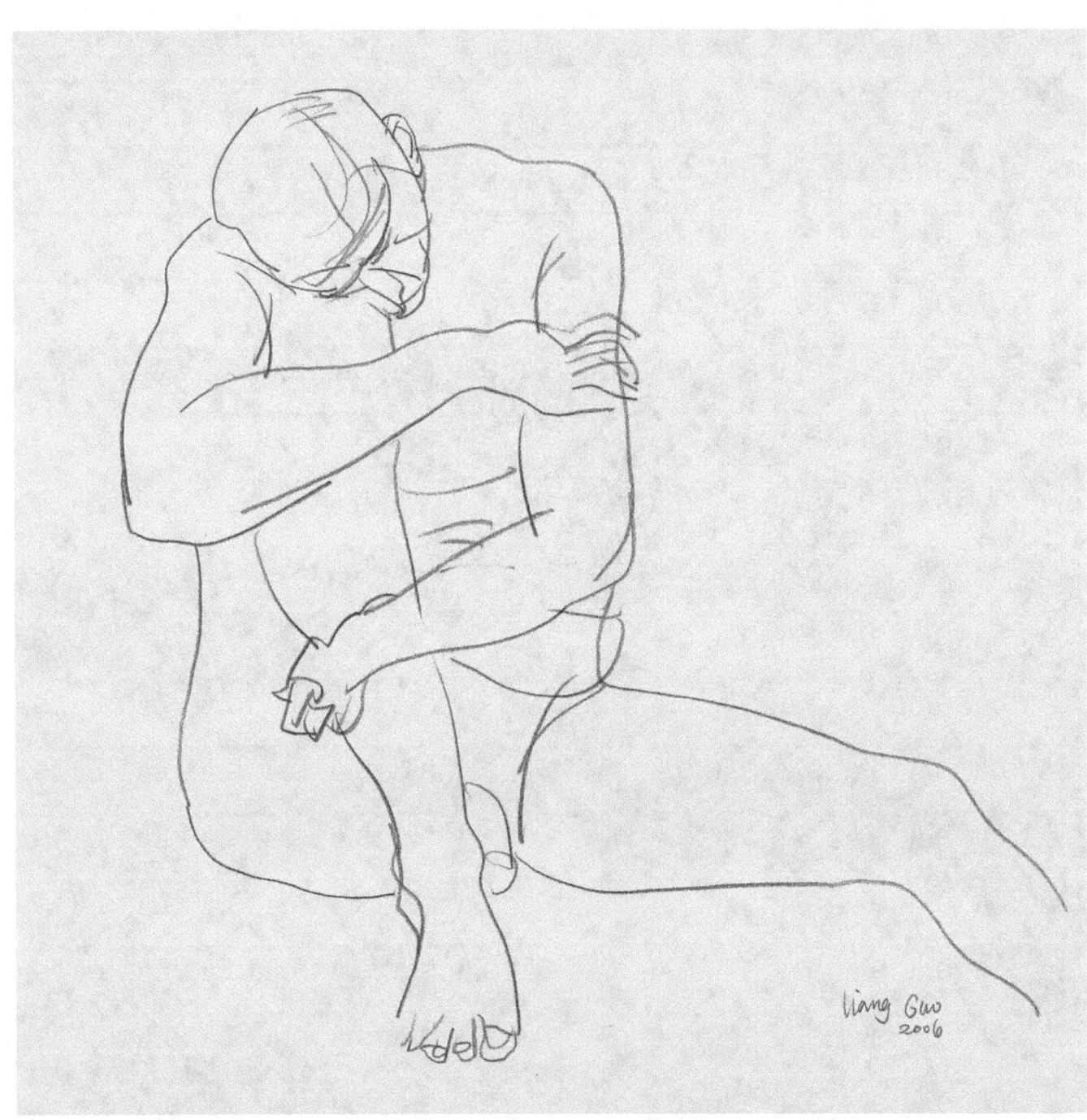

4   Dawn, 2006, Pencil

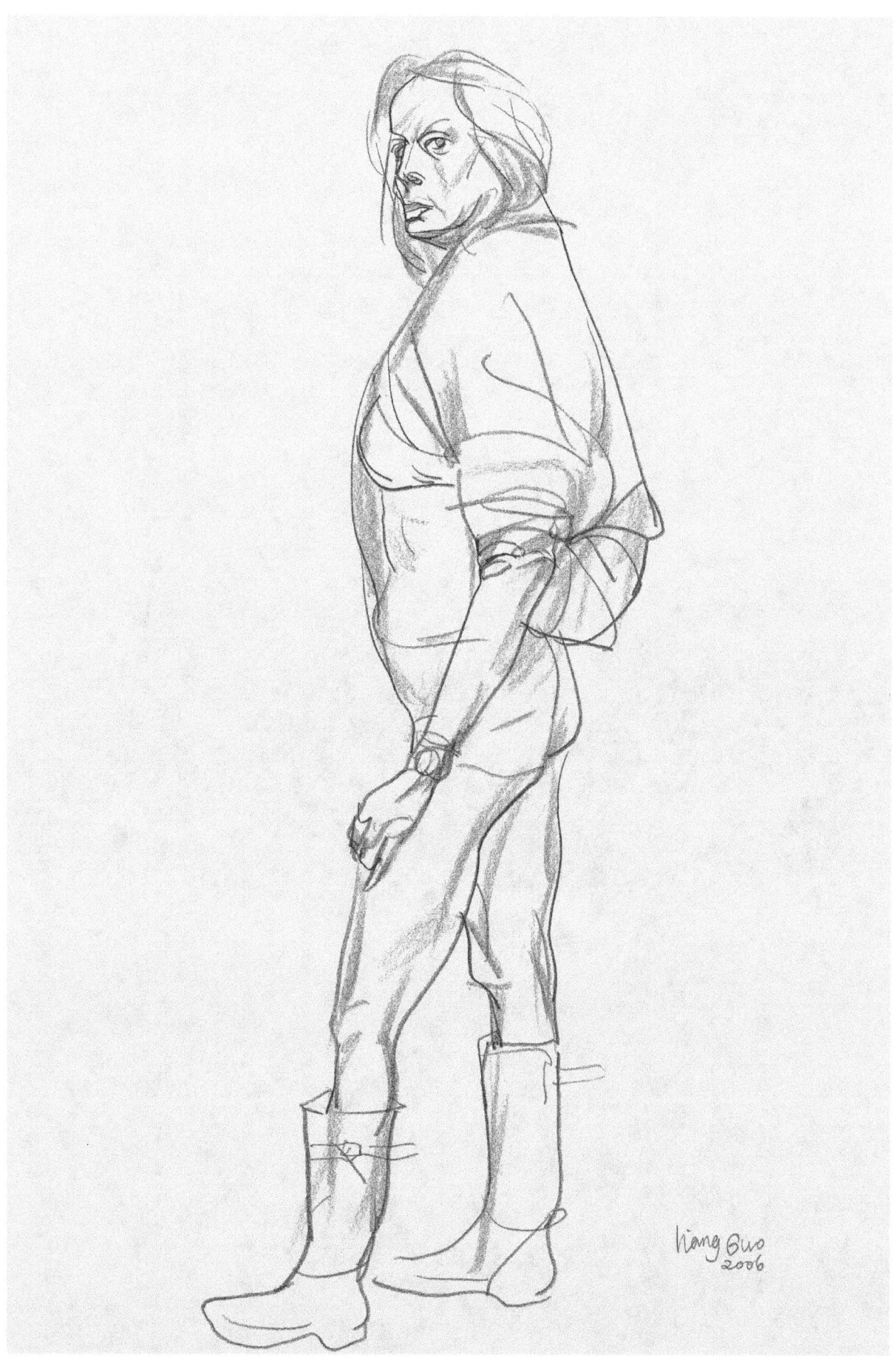

5    Making fashion, 2006, Pencil and charcoal

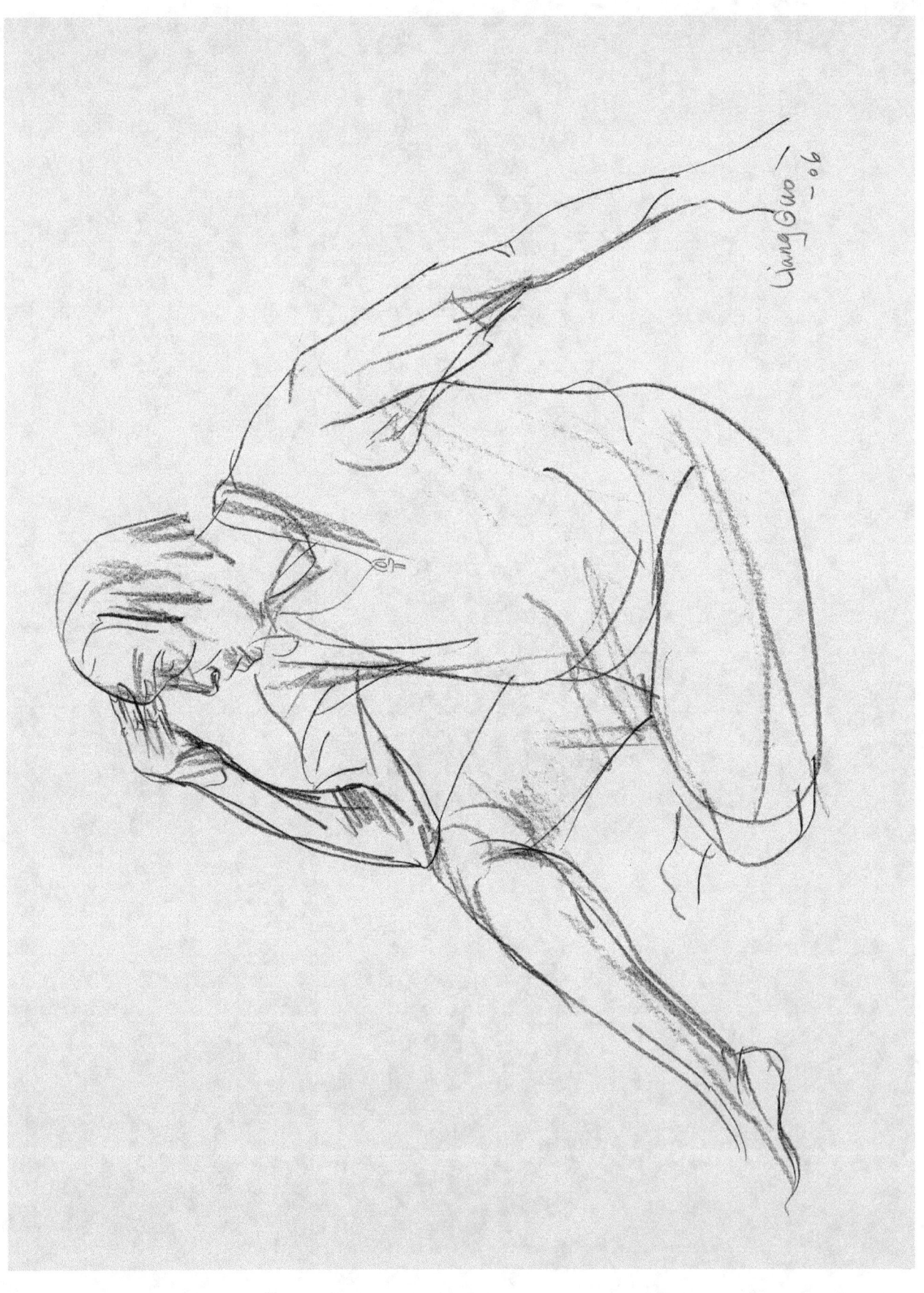

6    Under consideration, 2006, Charcoal

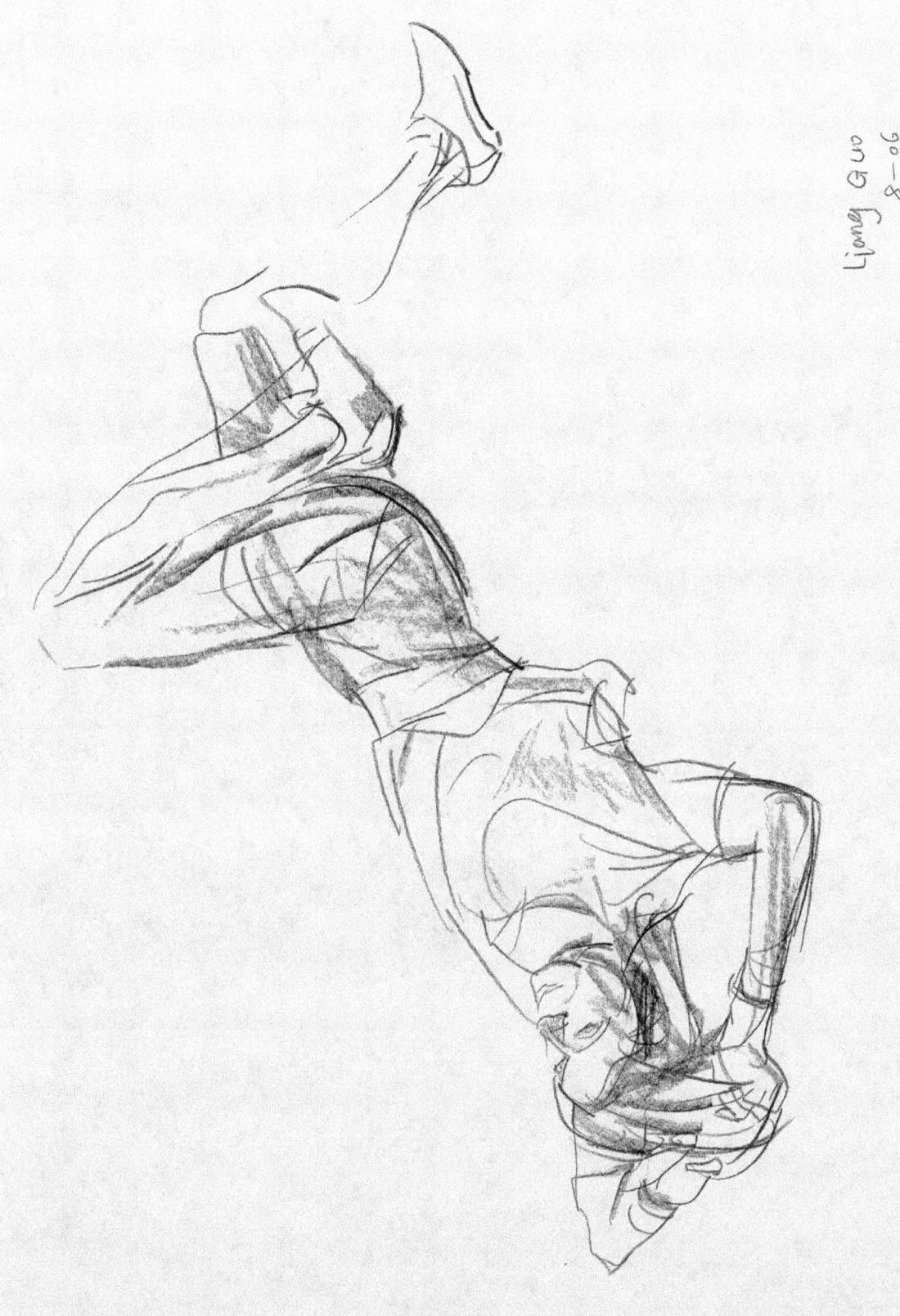

Liang Guo
8—06

7 Making choices, 2006, Charcoal

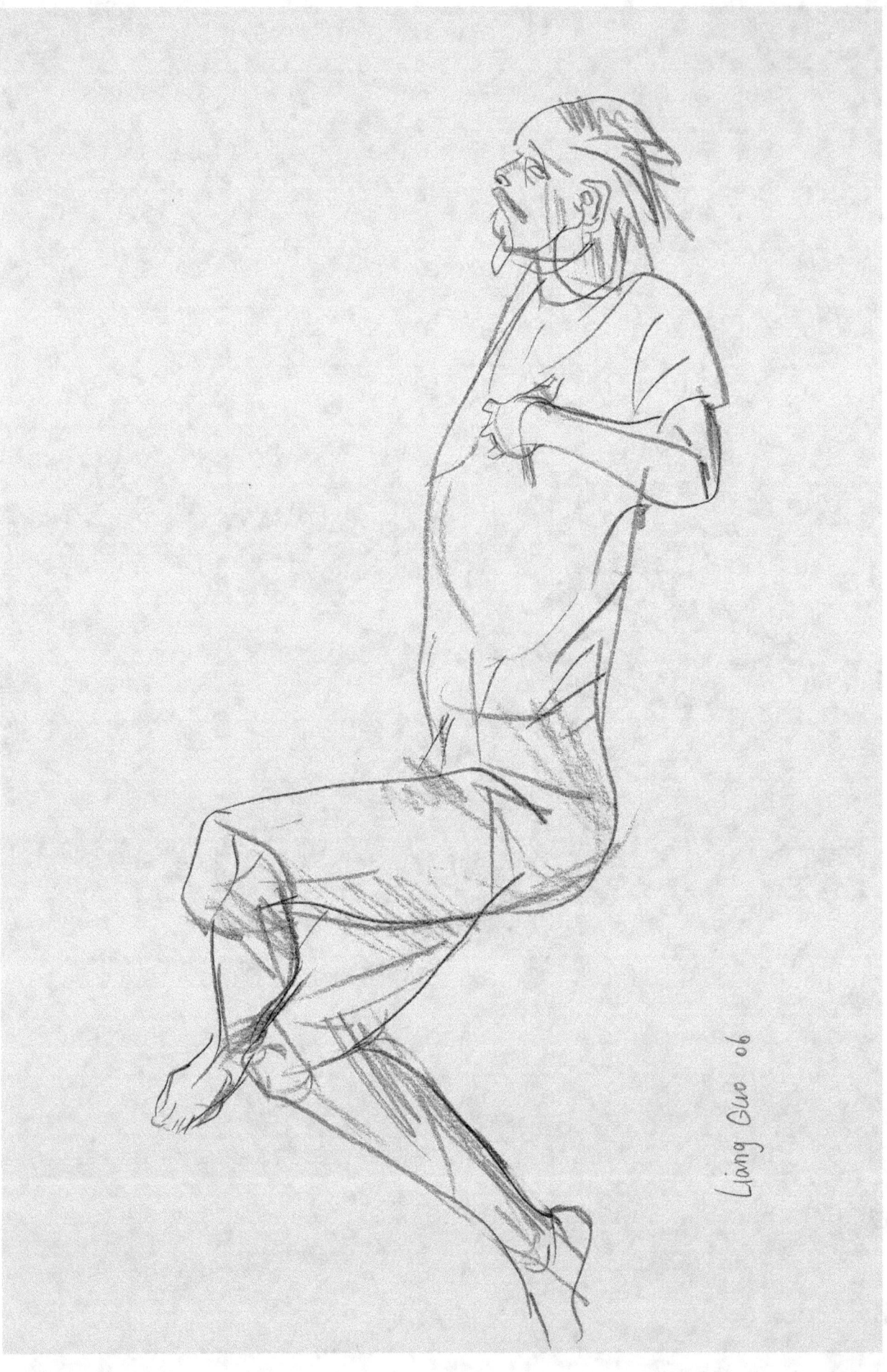

Liang Guo 06

8    Relaxing, 2006, Charcoal

Wang Guo
2006

9   Balance, 2006, Pencil

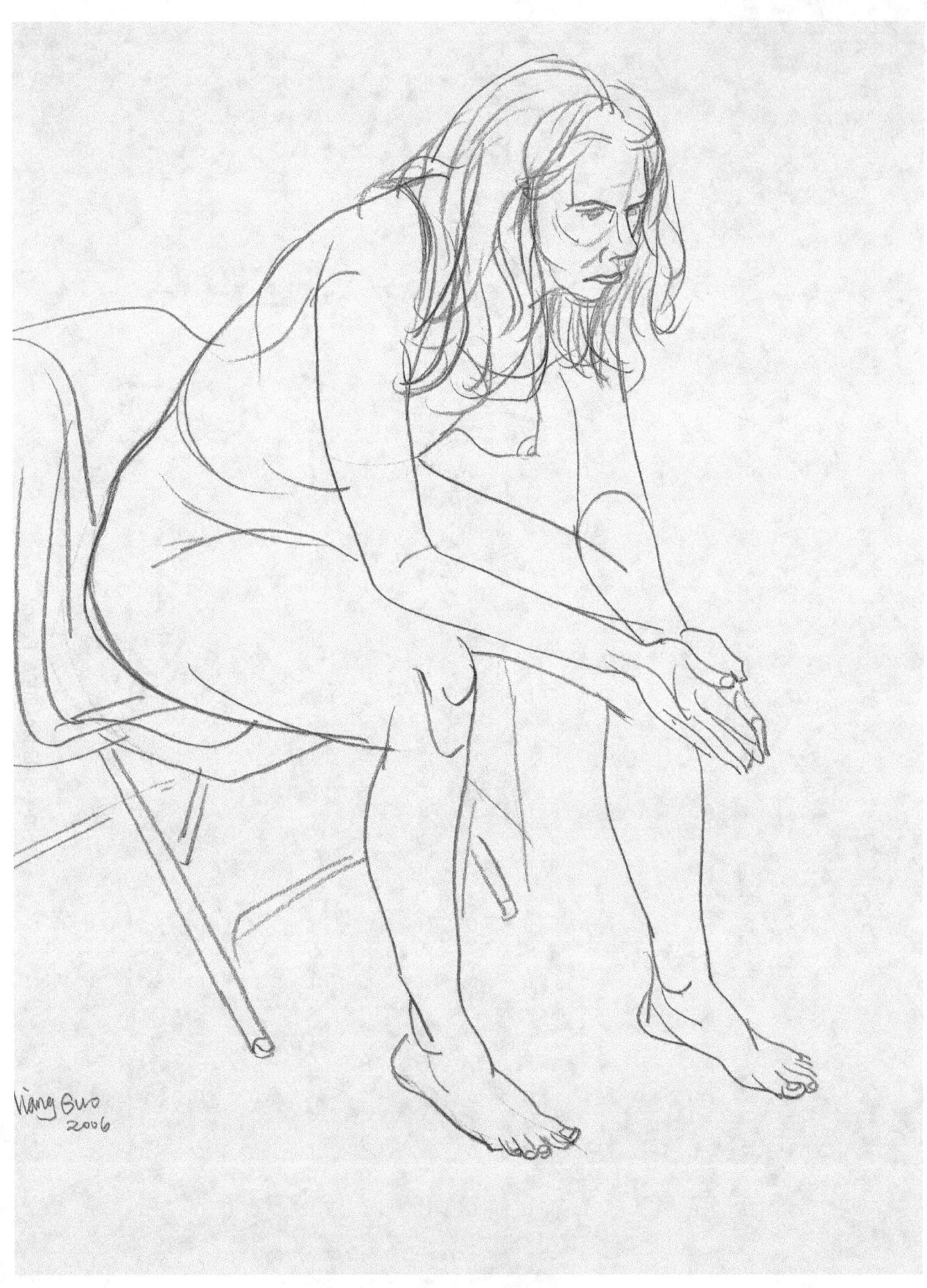

10    Touch the right chord, 2006, Pencil

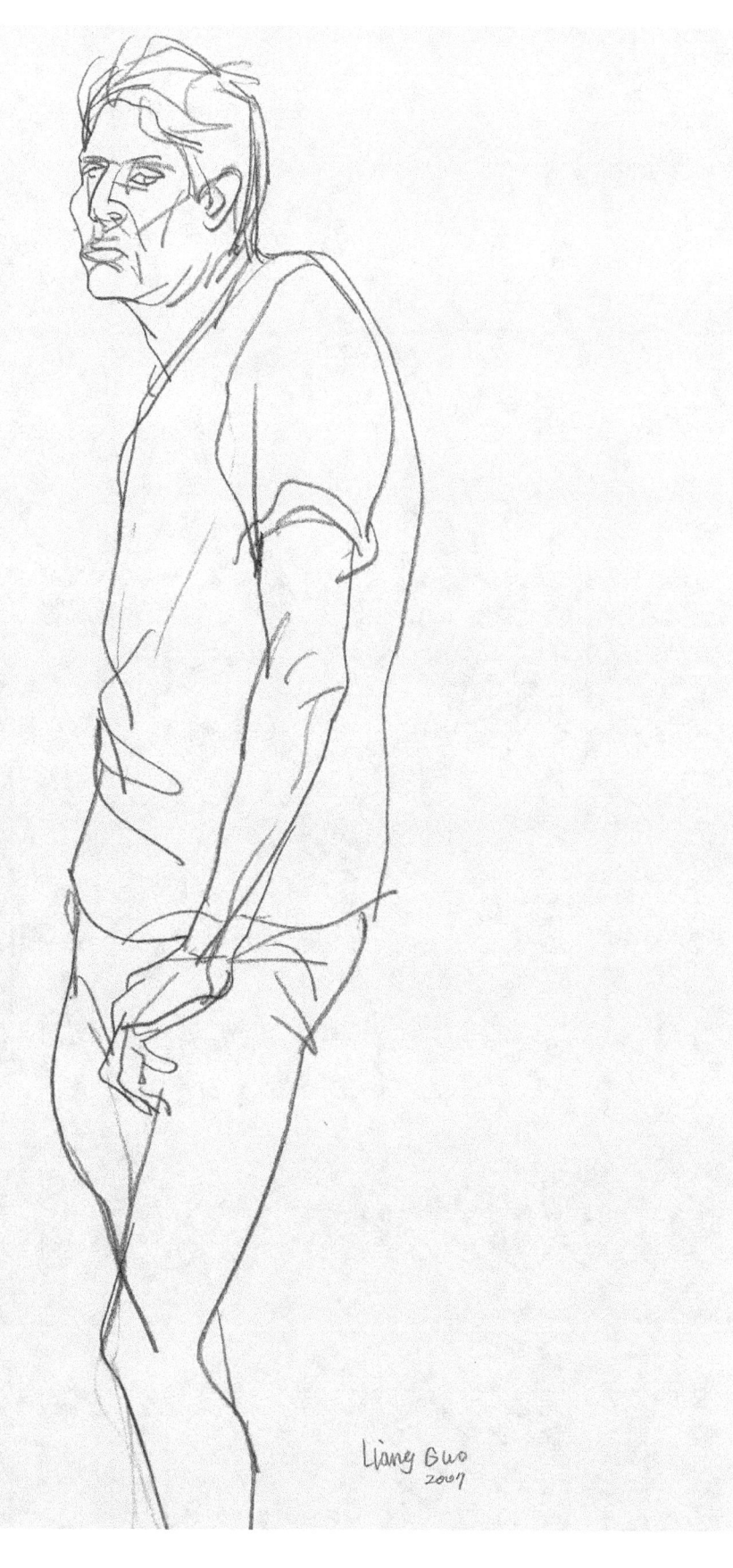

11    Regret, 2007, Pencil

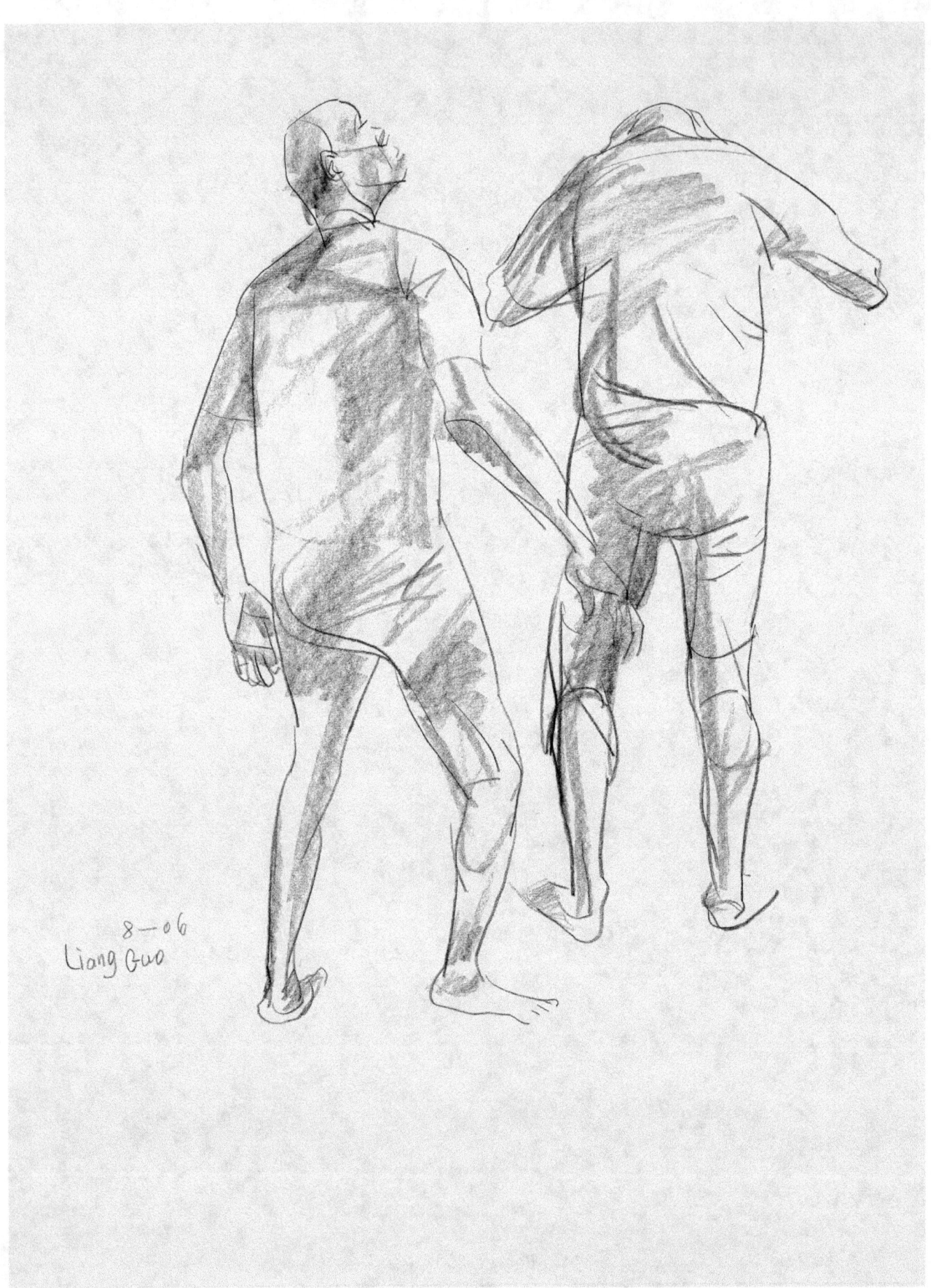

8—06
Liang Guo

12    Where is the wind from, 2006, Monolith pencil

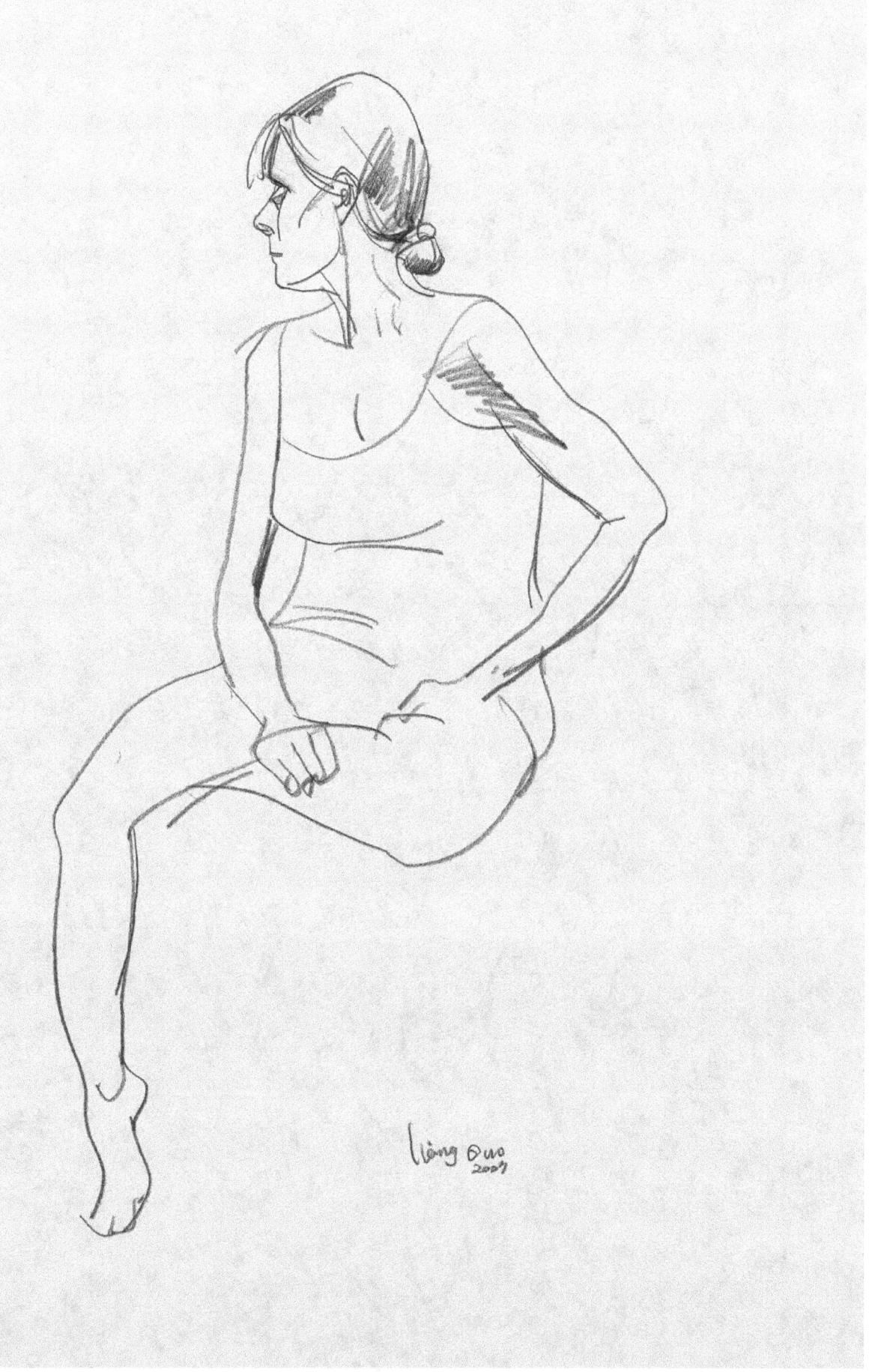

13    Straight forward, 2007, Charcoal

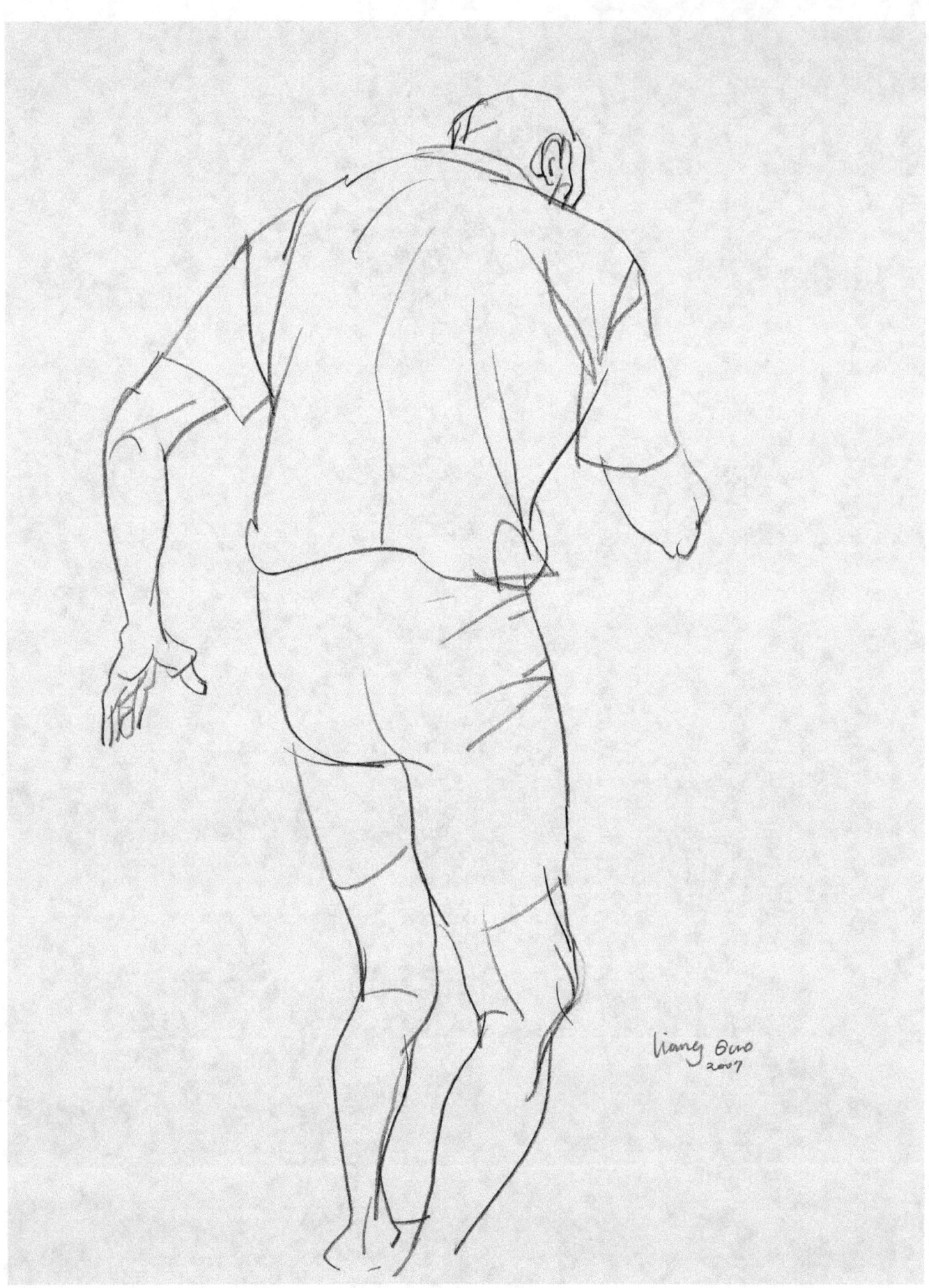

14    Water on the floor, 2007, Pencil

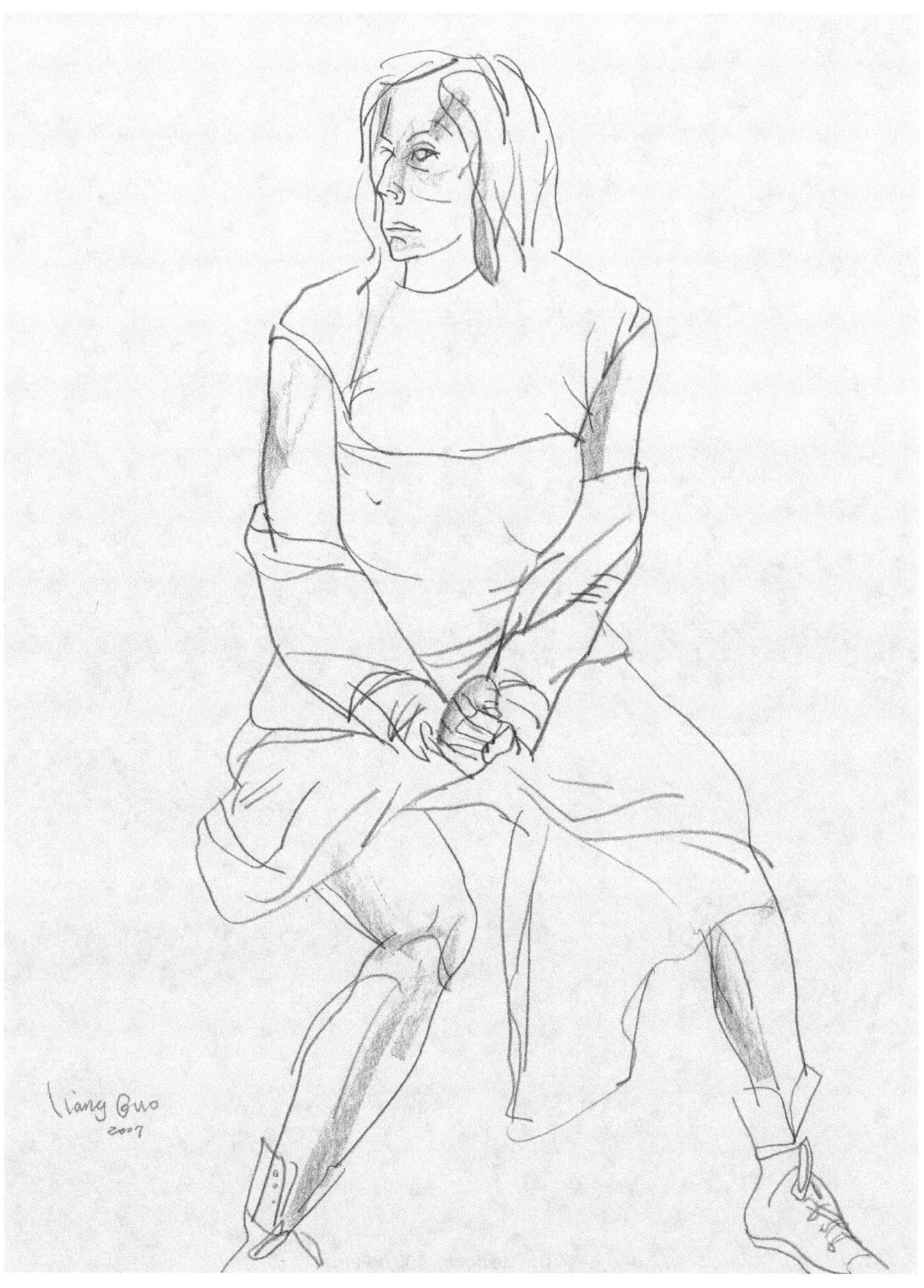

15    How can I know, 2007, Monolith pencil

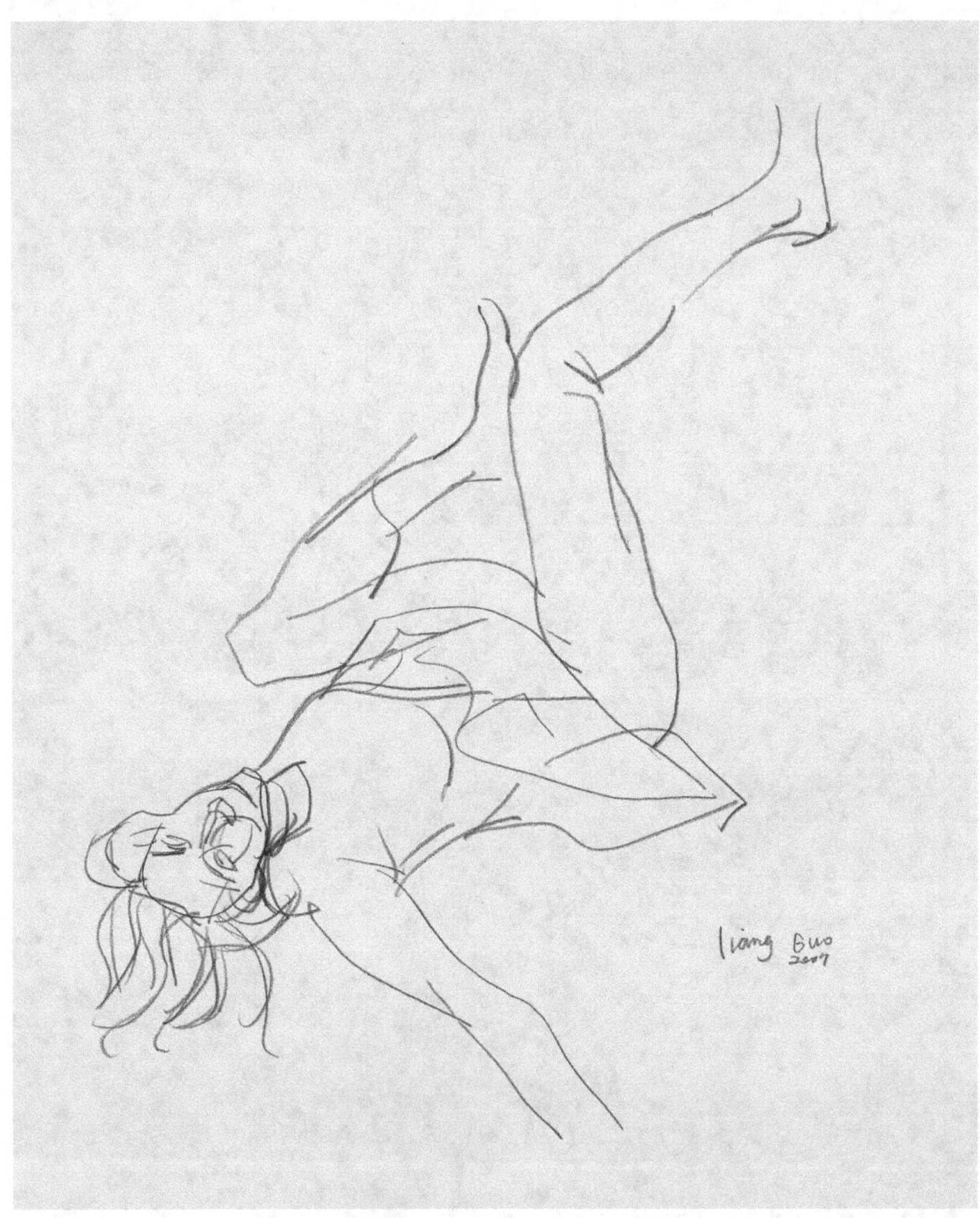

16    Upside down, 2007, Pencil

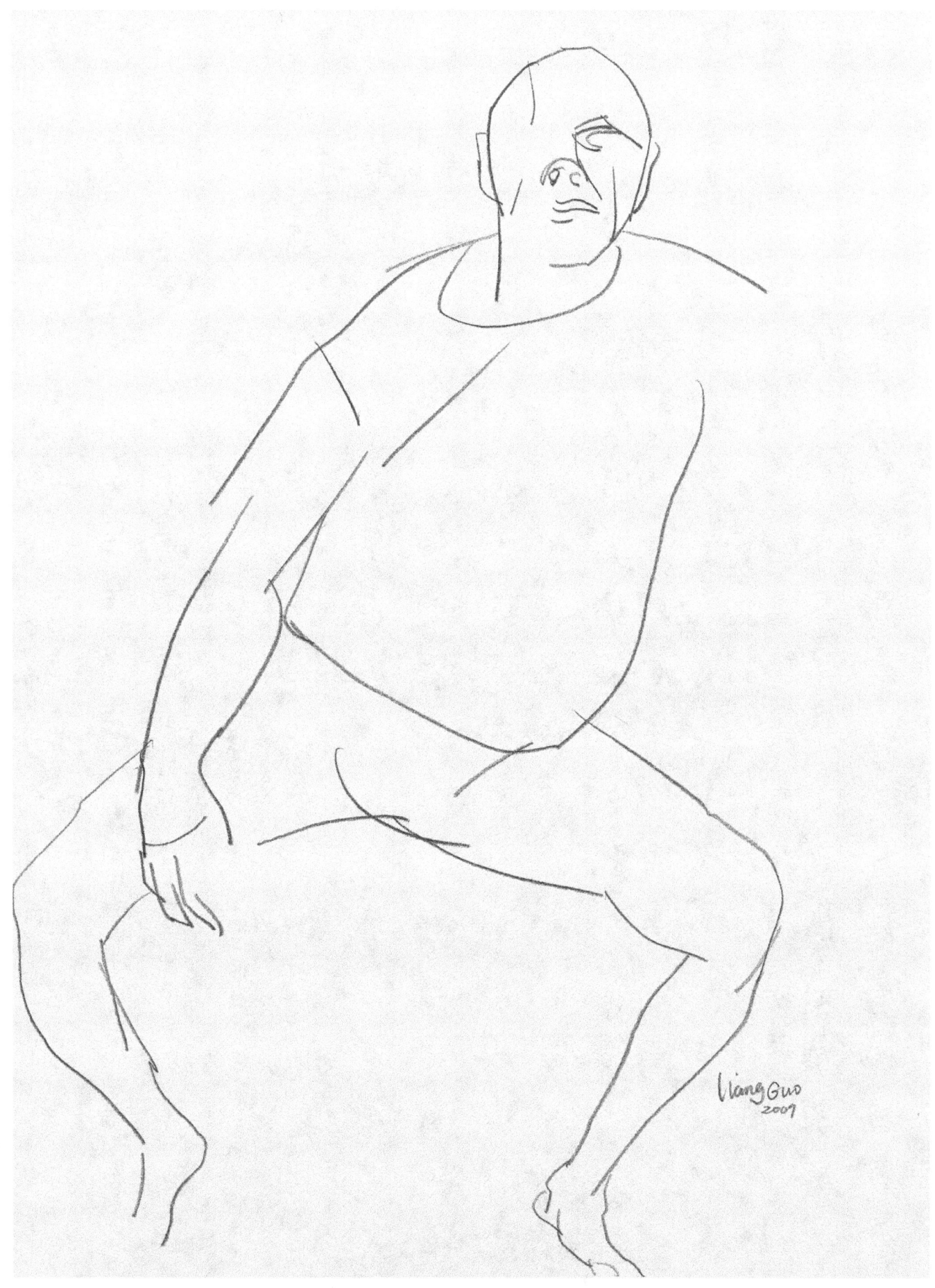

17    Without awareness, 2007, Pencil

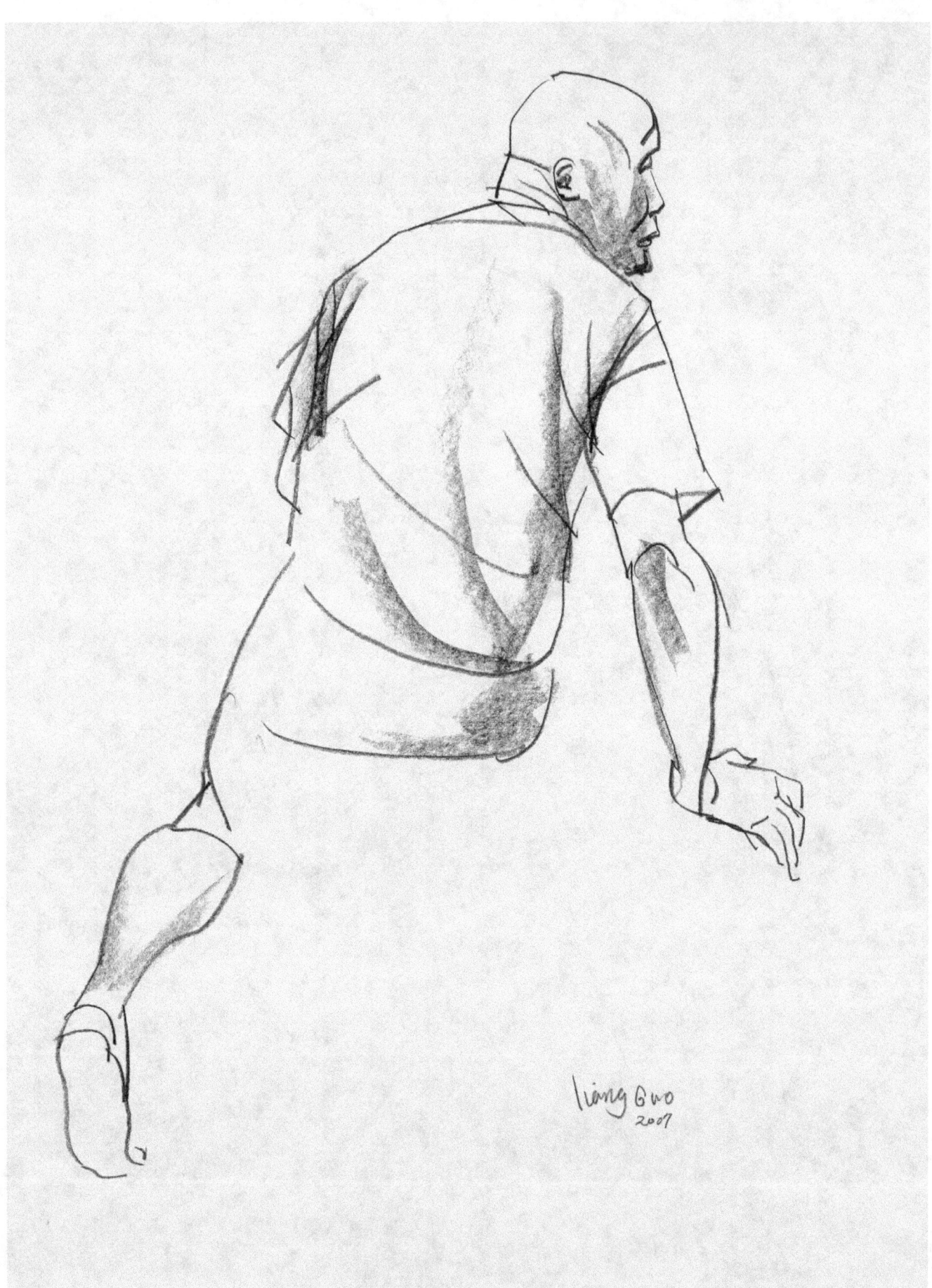

18    Twist, 2007, Pencil and charcoal

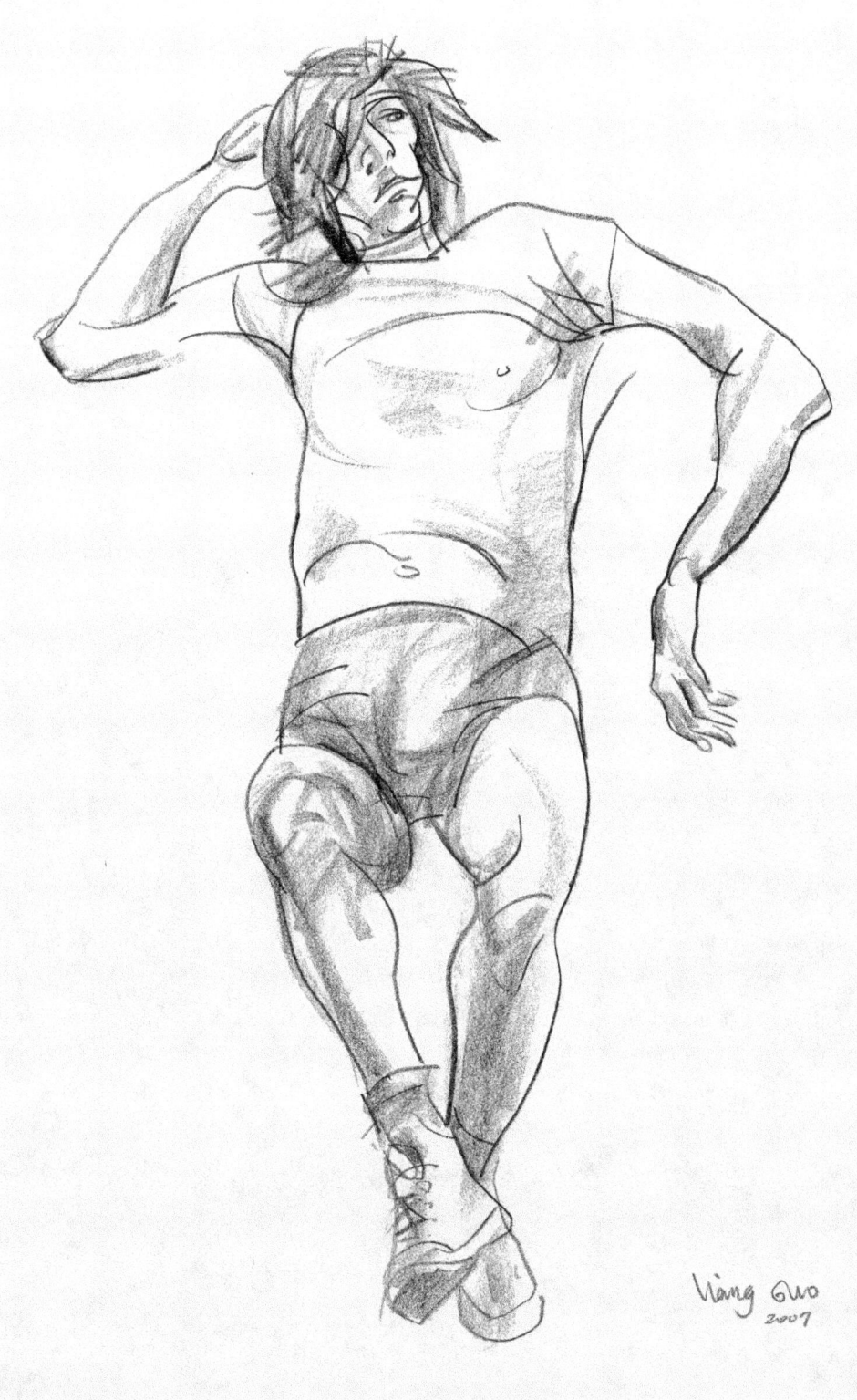

19     Lean against, 2007, Pencil and charcoal

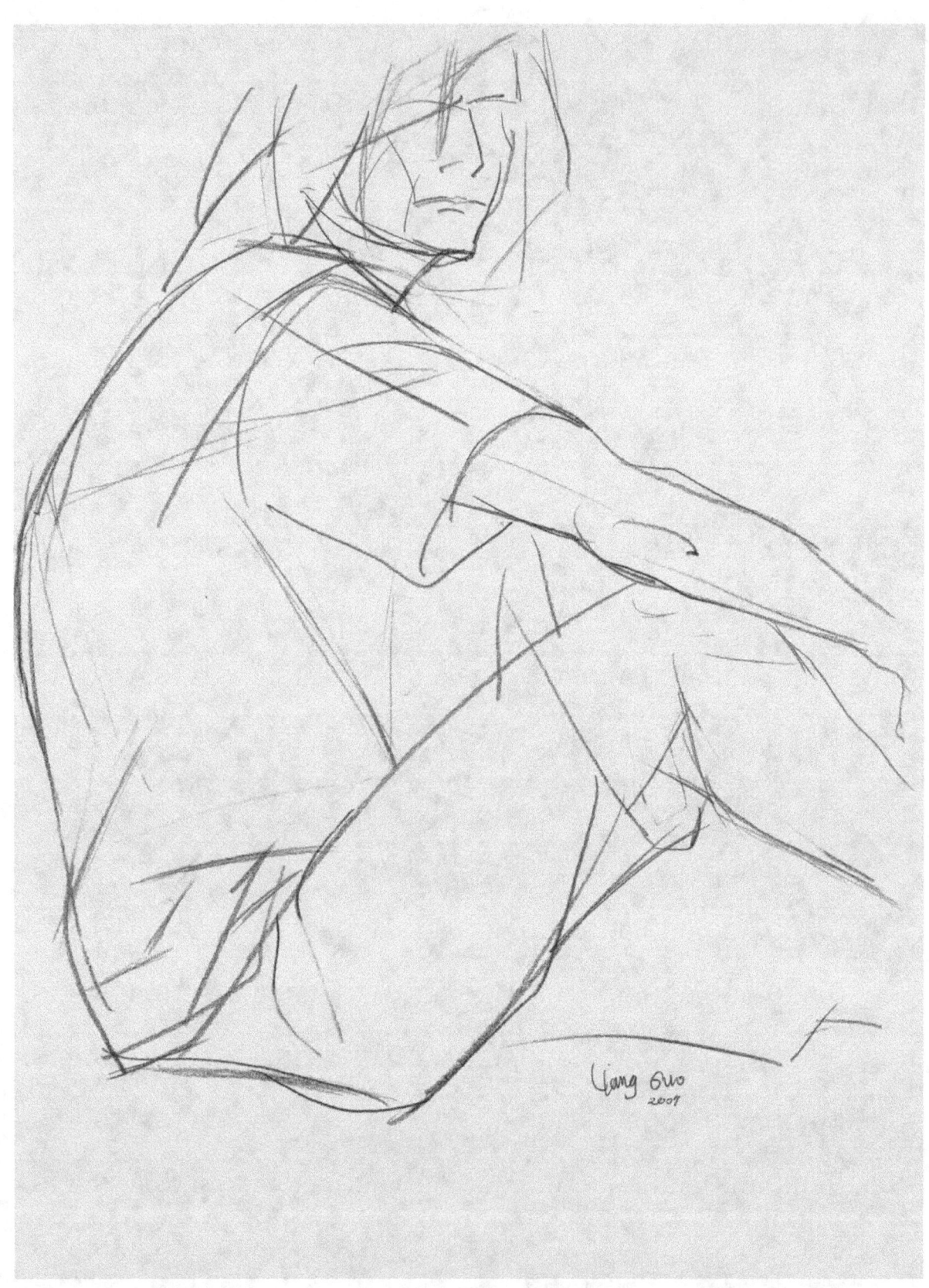

20    Hidden mind, 2007, Pencil

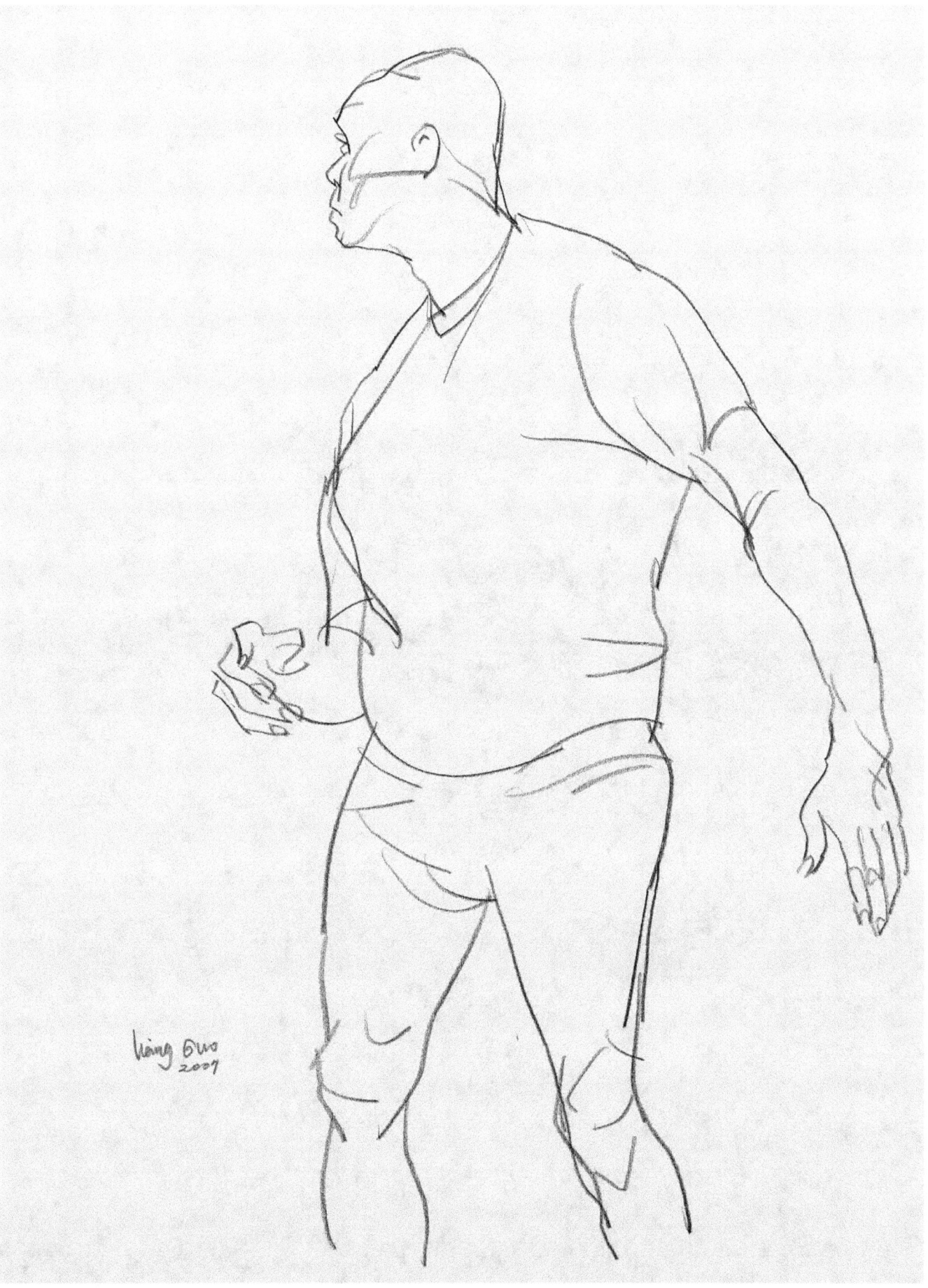

21    Old player, 2007, Pencil

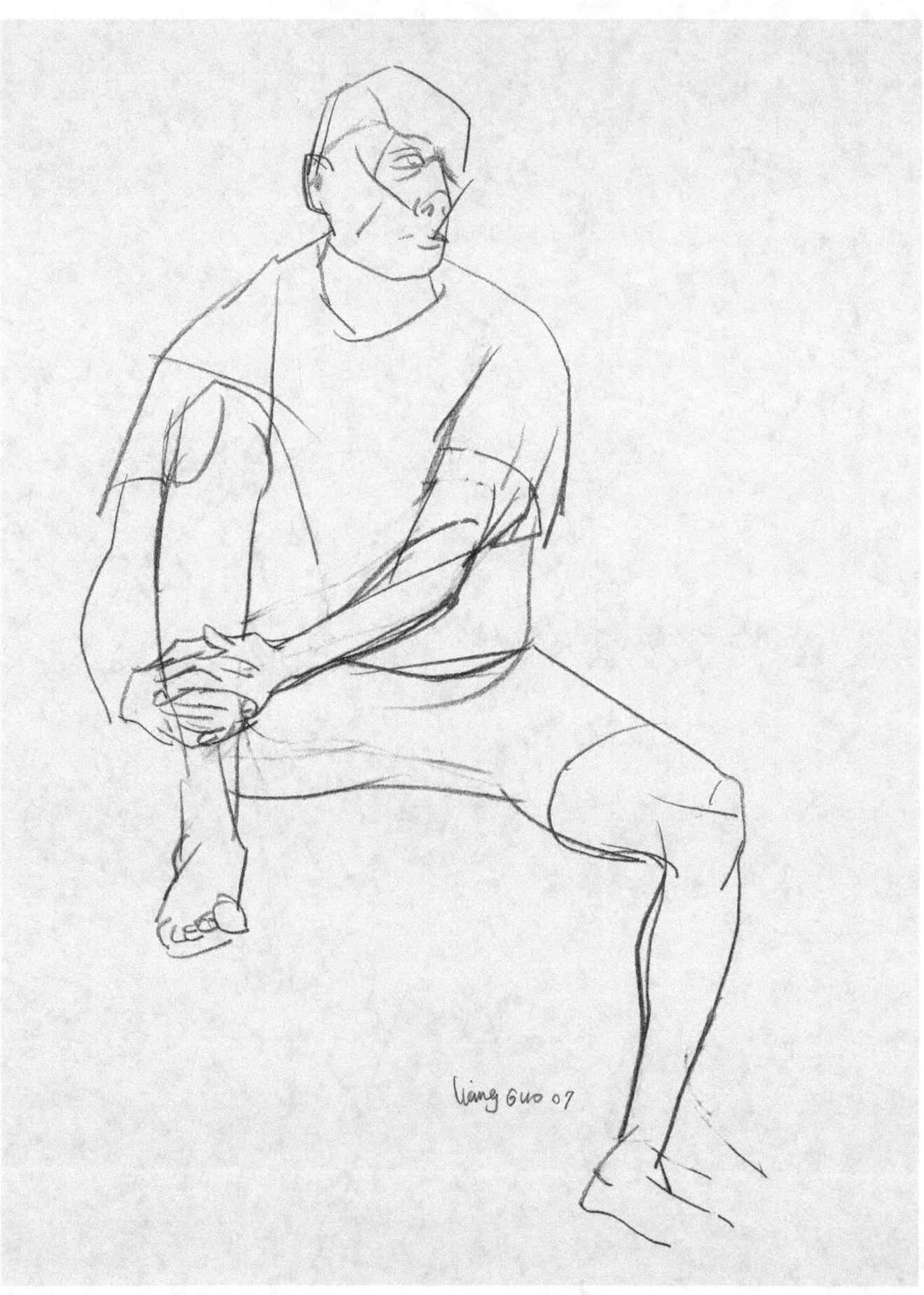

22    Routine, 2007, Pencil

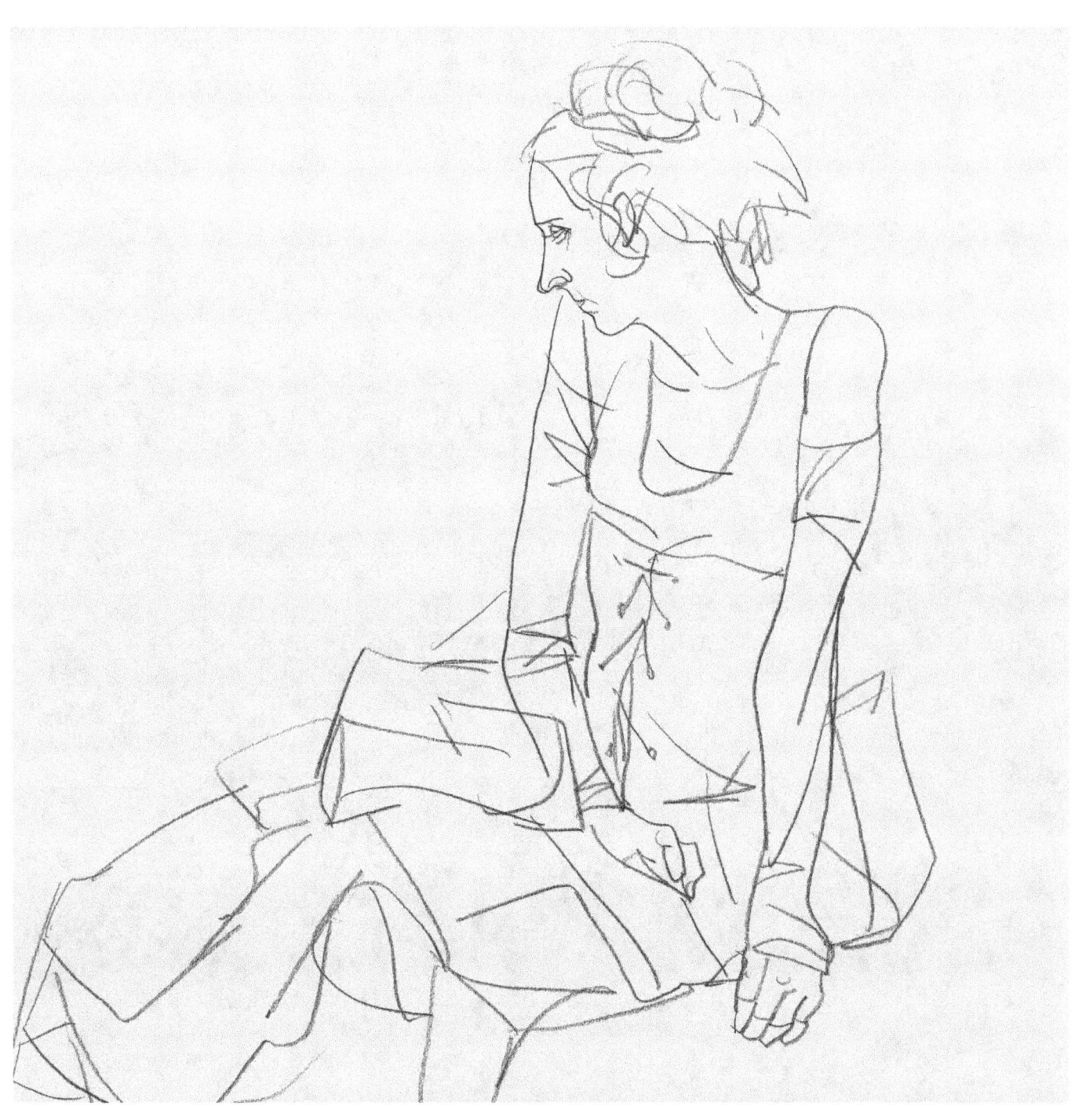

23    New dress, 2007, Pencil

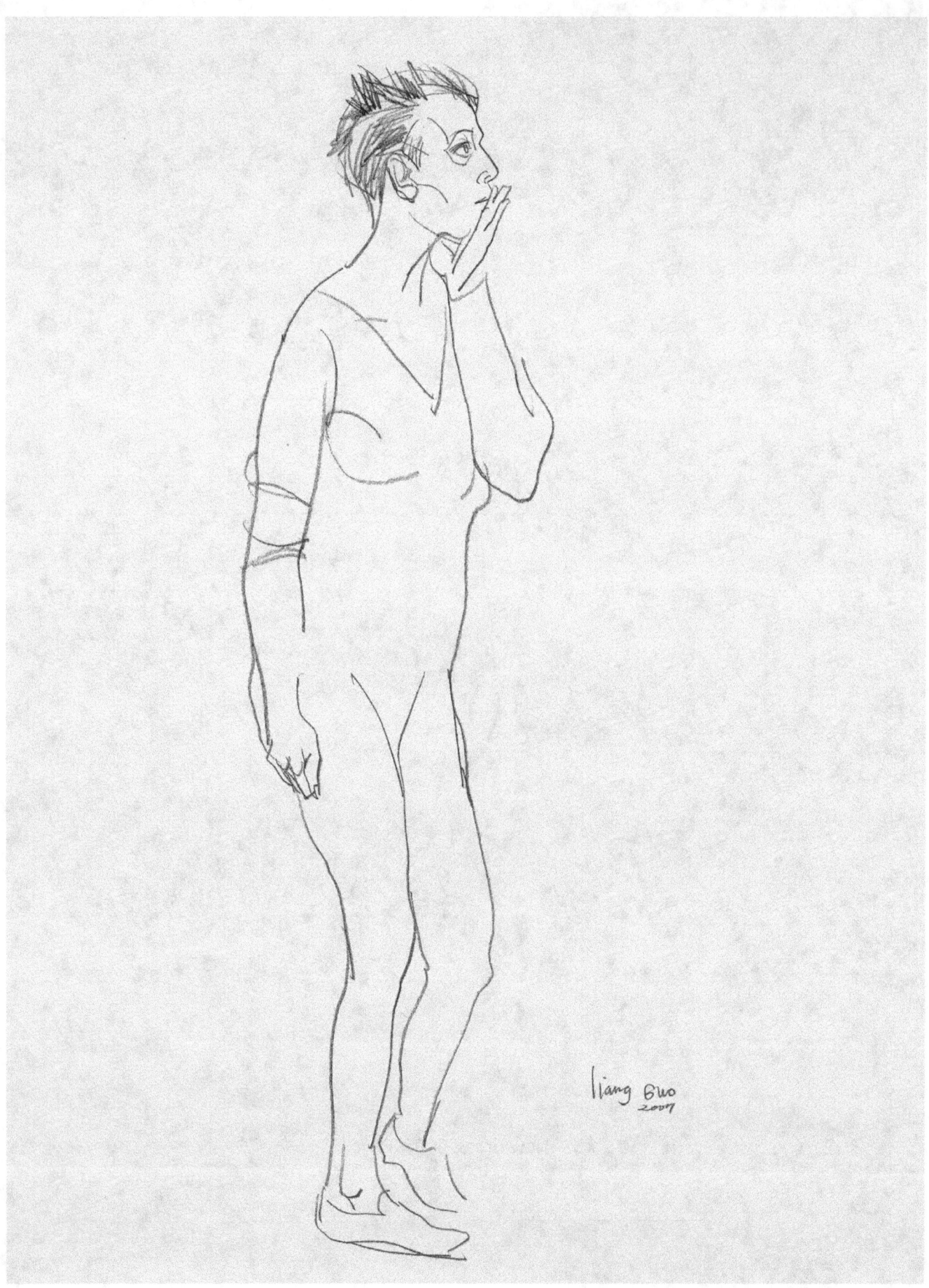

24    Fifty-fifty, 2007, Pencil

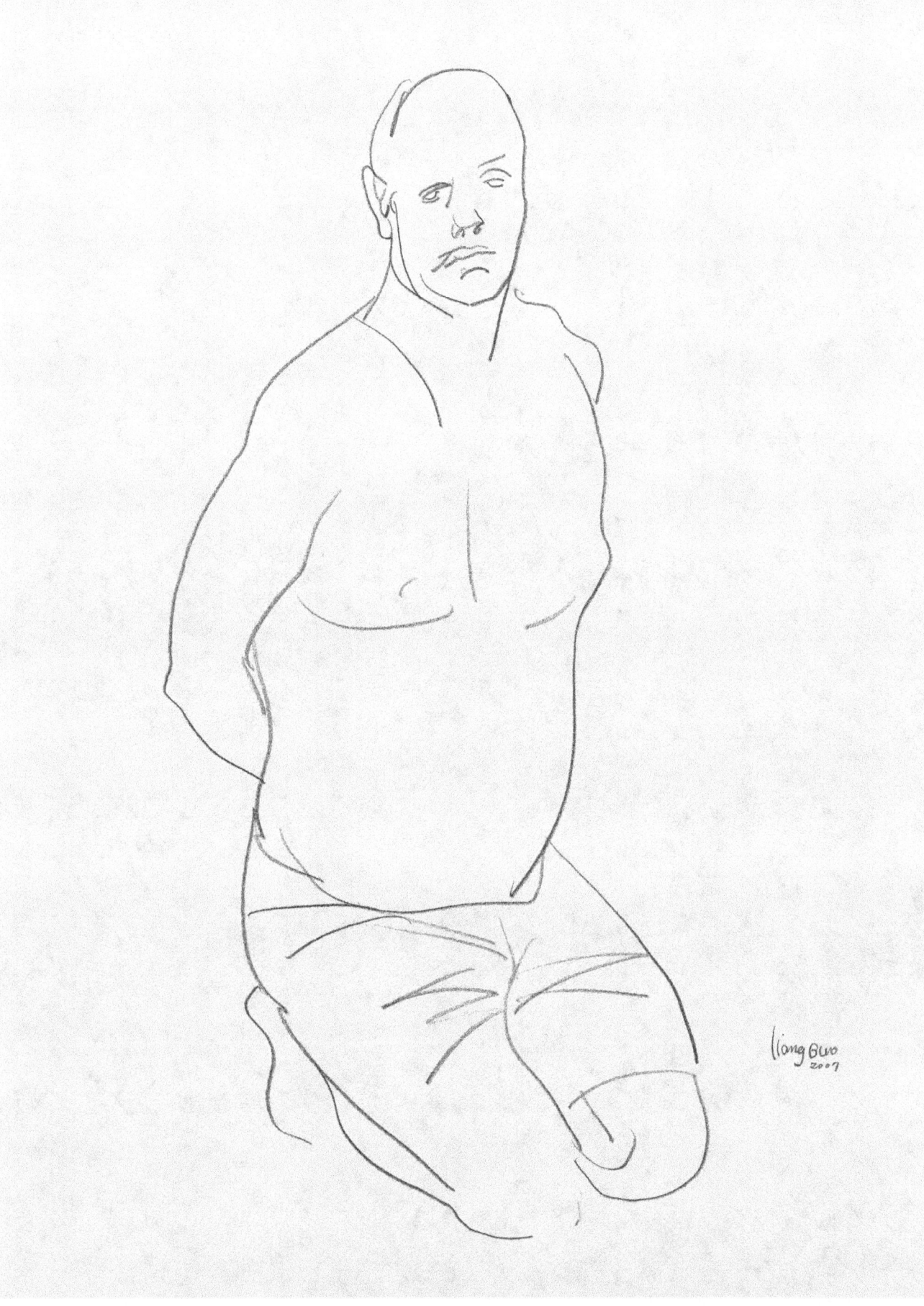

25    By the river, 2007, Pencil

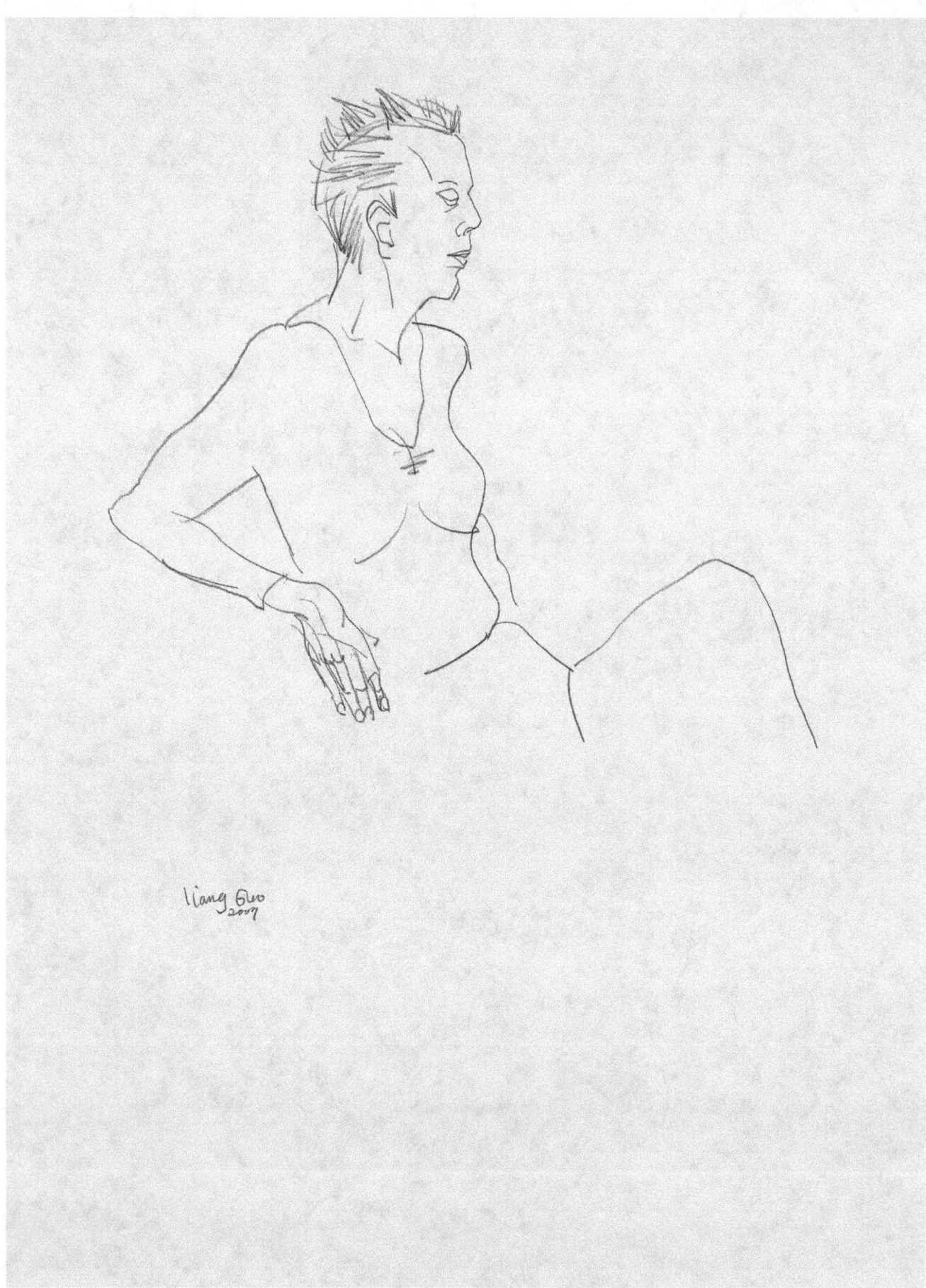

26    Absence, 2007, Pencil

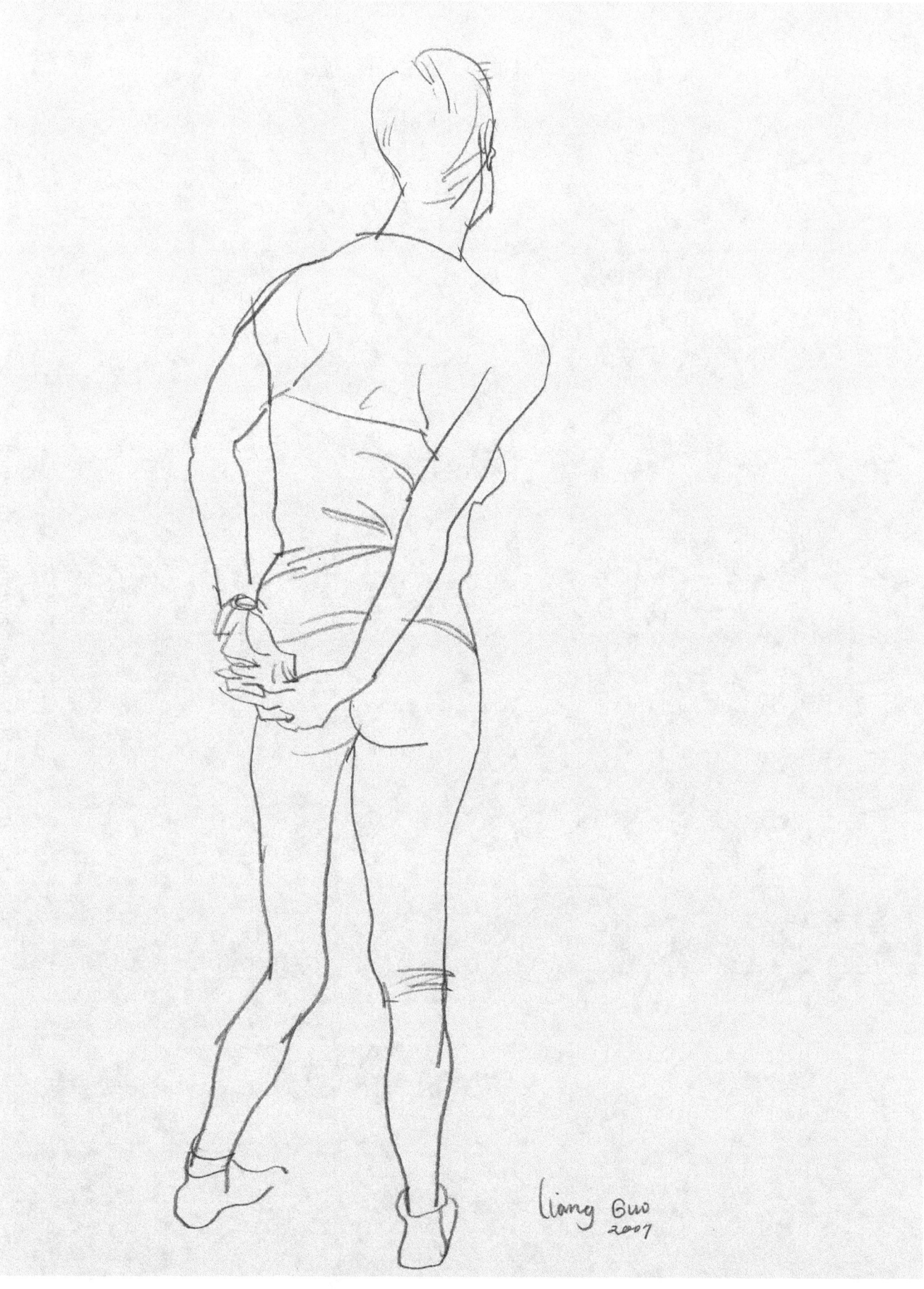

27    Wondering, 2007, Pencil

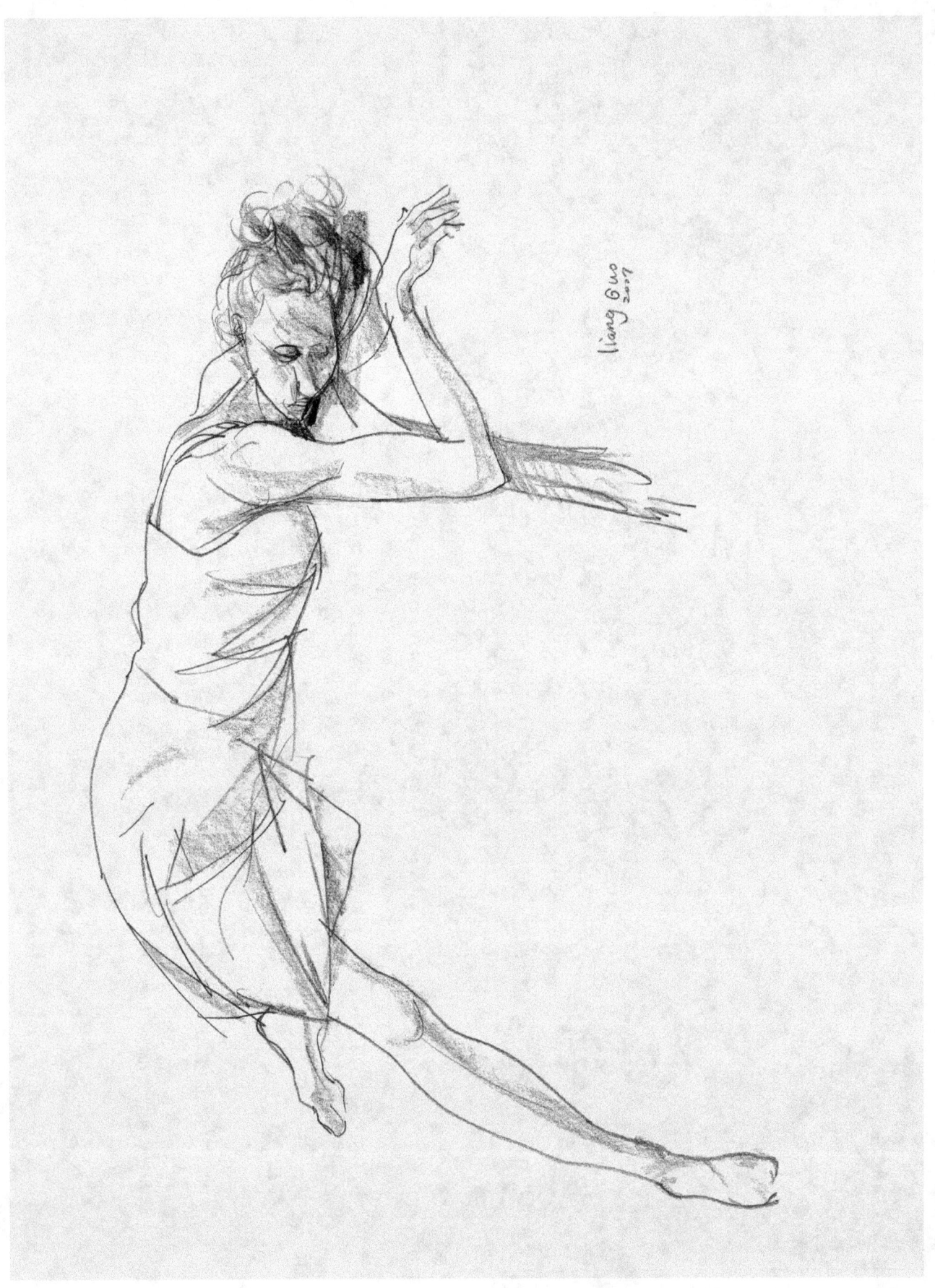

28   Daylight, 2007, Pencil and monolith pencil

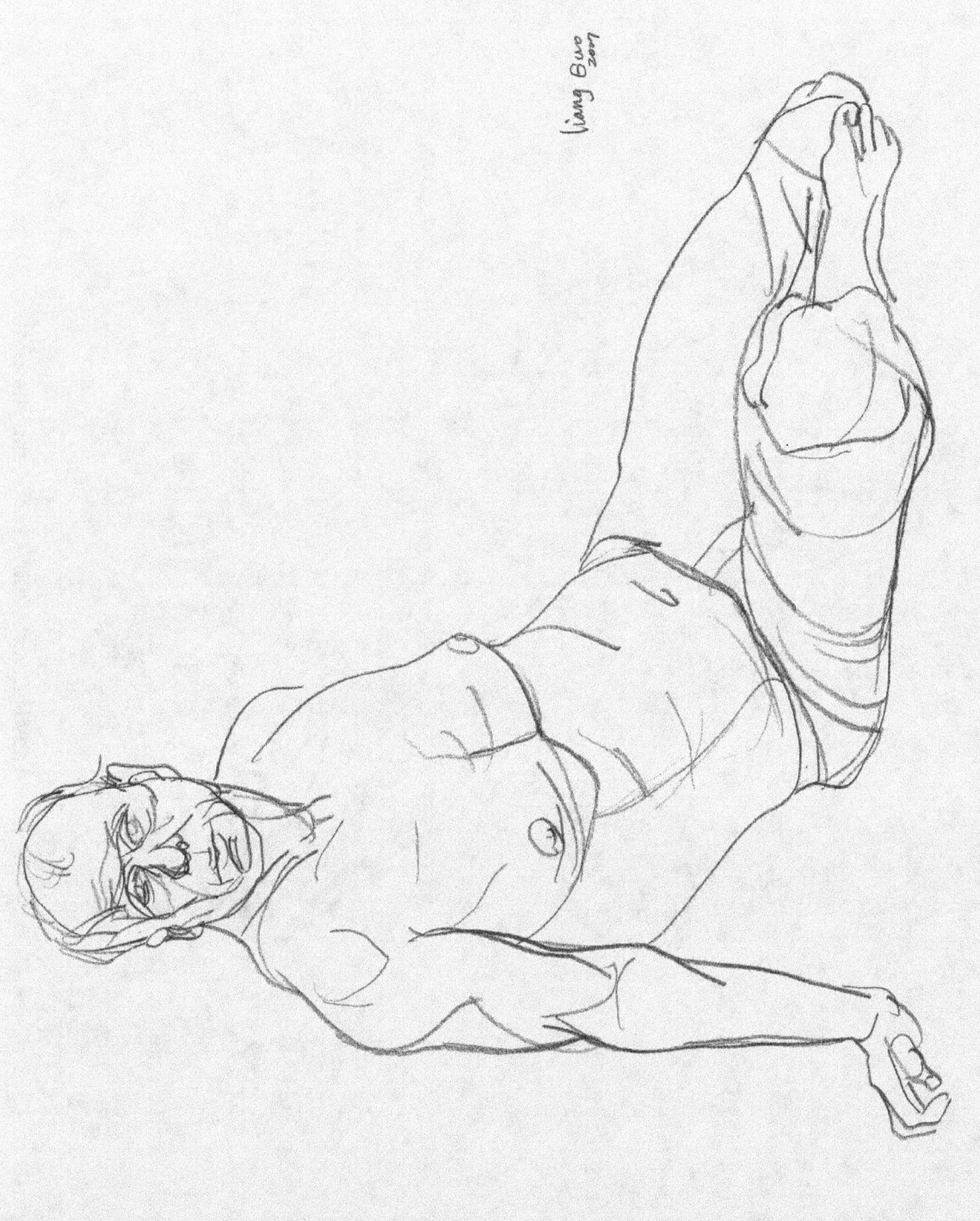

29    Moved by the story, 2007, Charcoal

30   Lady Network, 2007, Pencil and charcoal

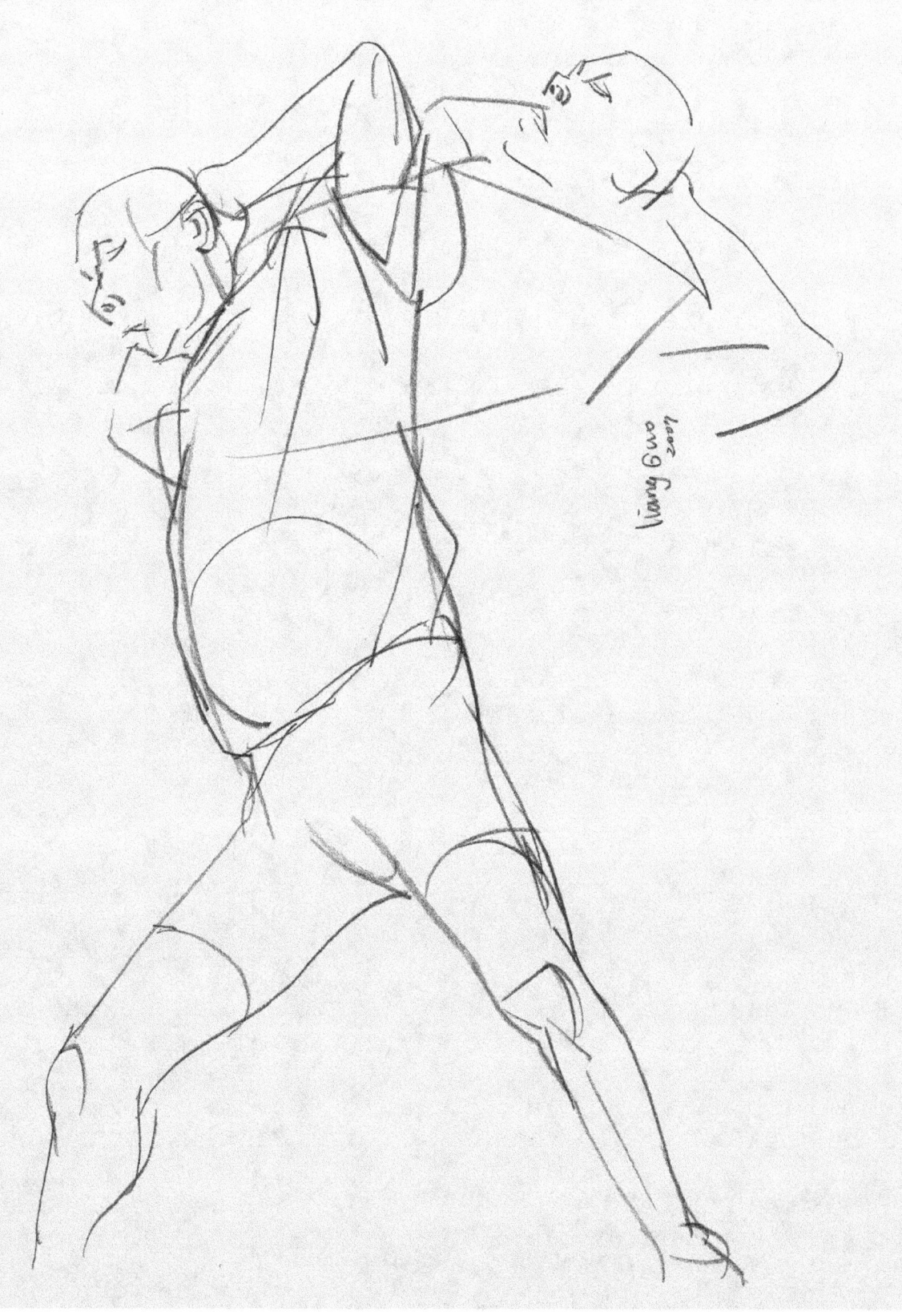

31    Escapist, 2007, Pencil

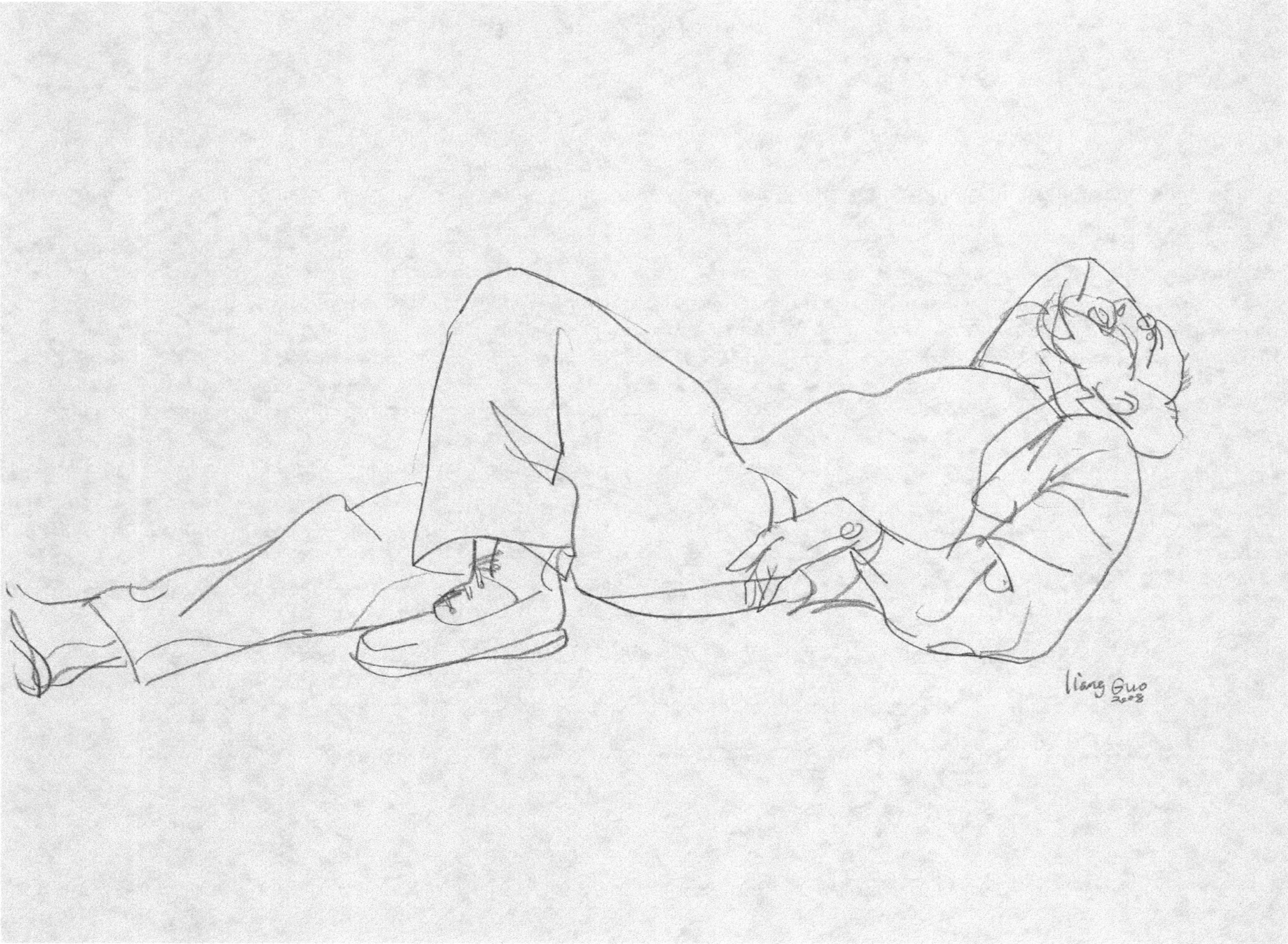


32 On a pleasant day, 2008, Pencil

33    Wait-and-see, 2008, Pencil

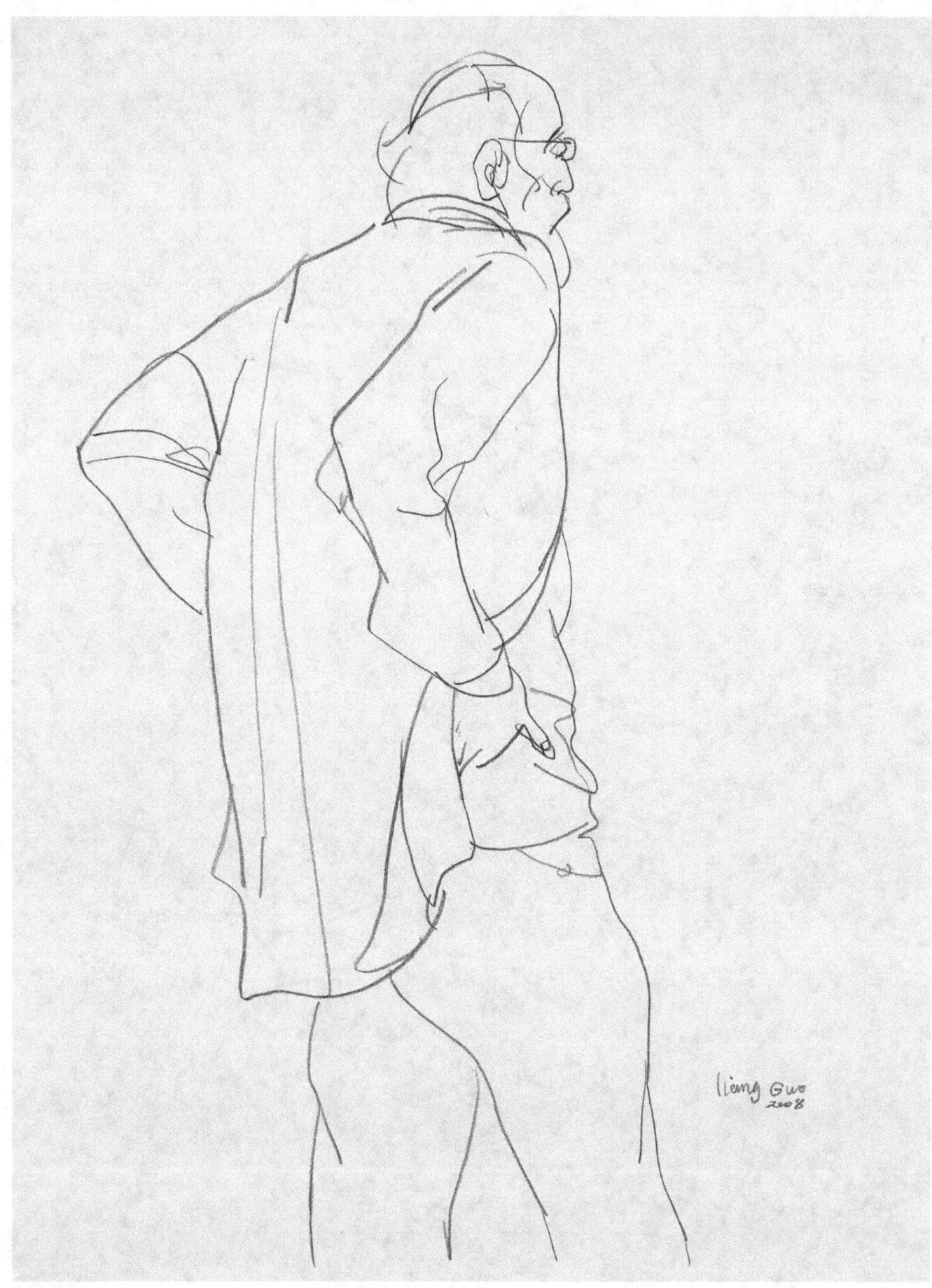

34　Gentleman, 2008, Pencil

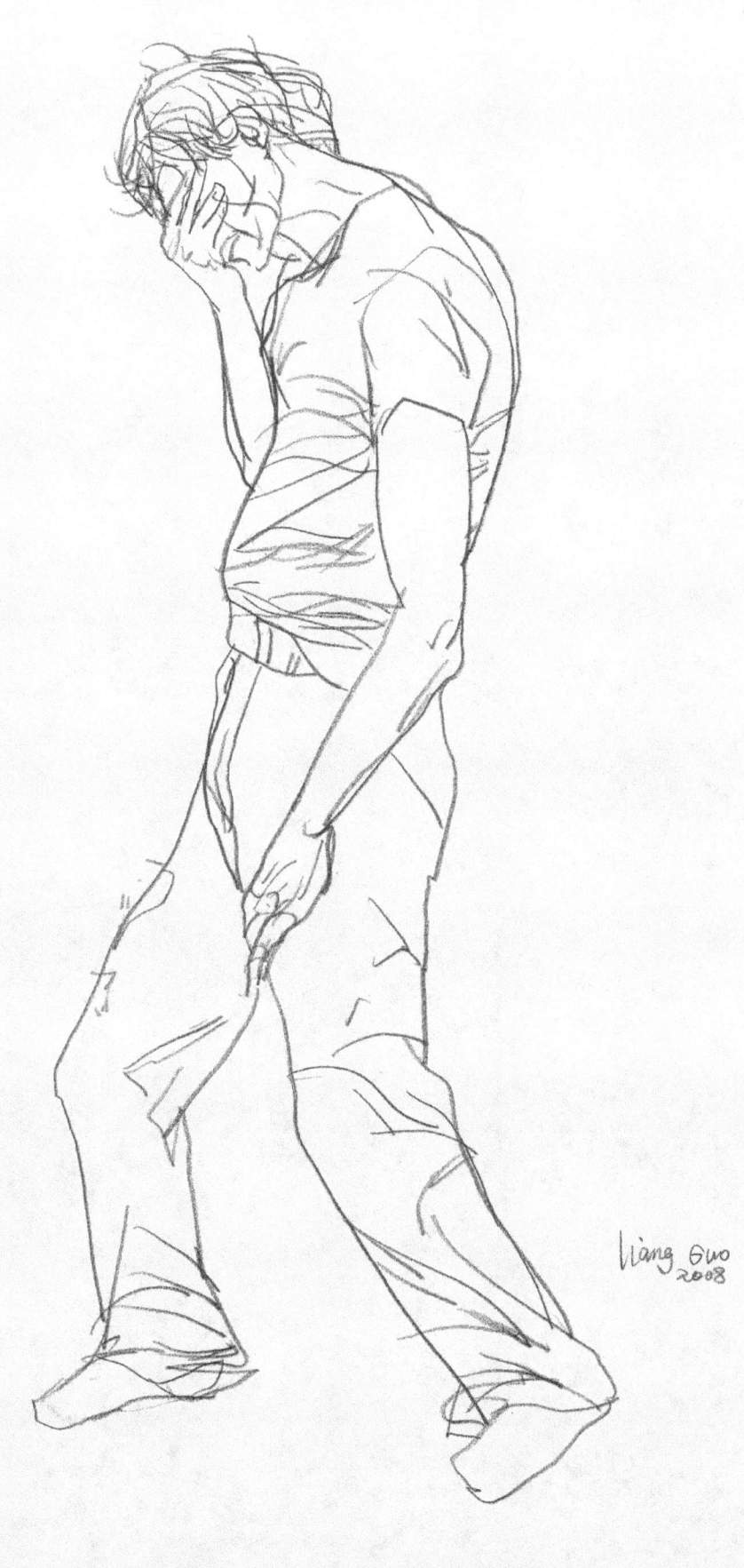

35    Past and present, 2008, Monolith pencil

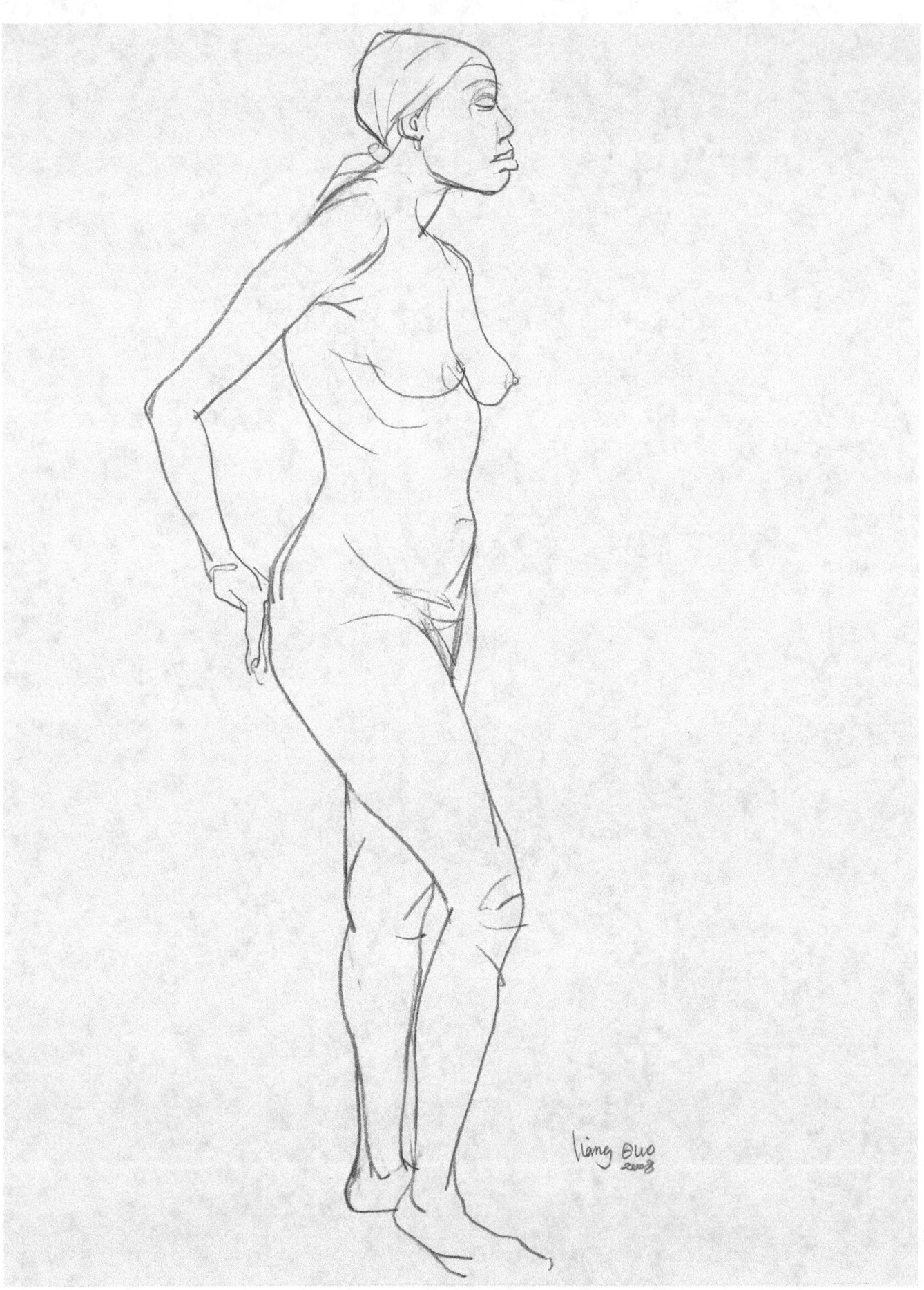

36    Hope,  2008, Pencil

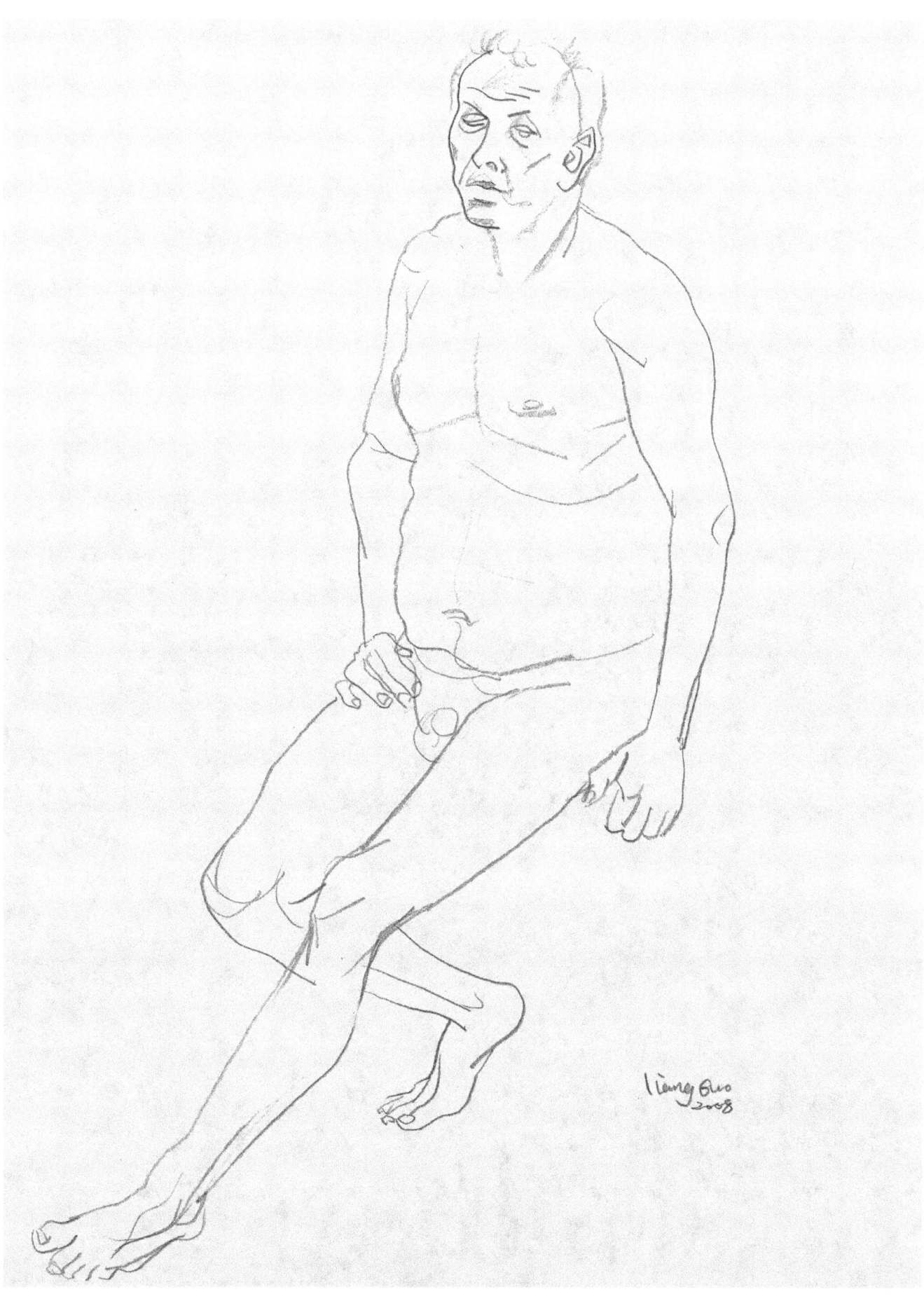

37    Positive attitude, 2008, Pencil

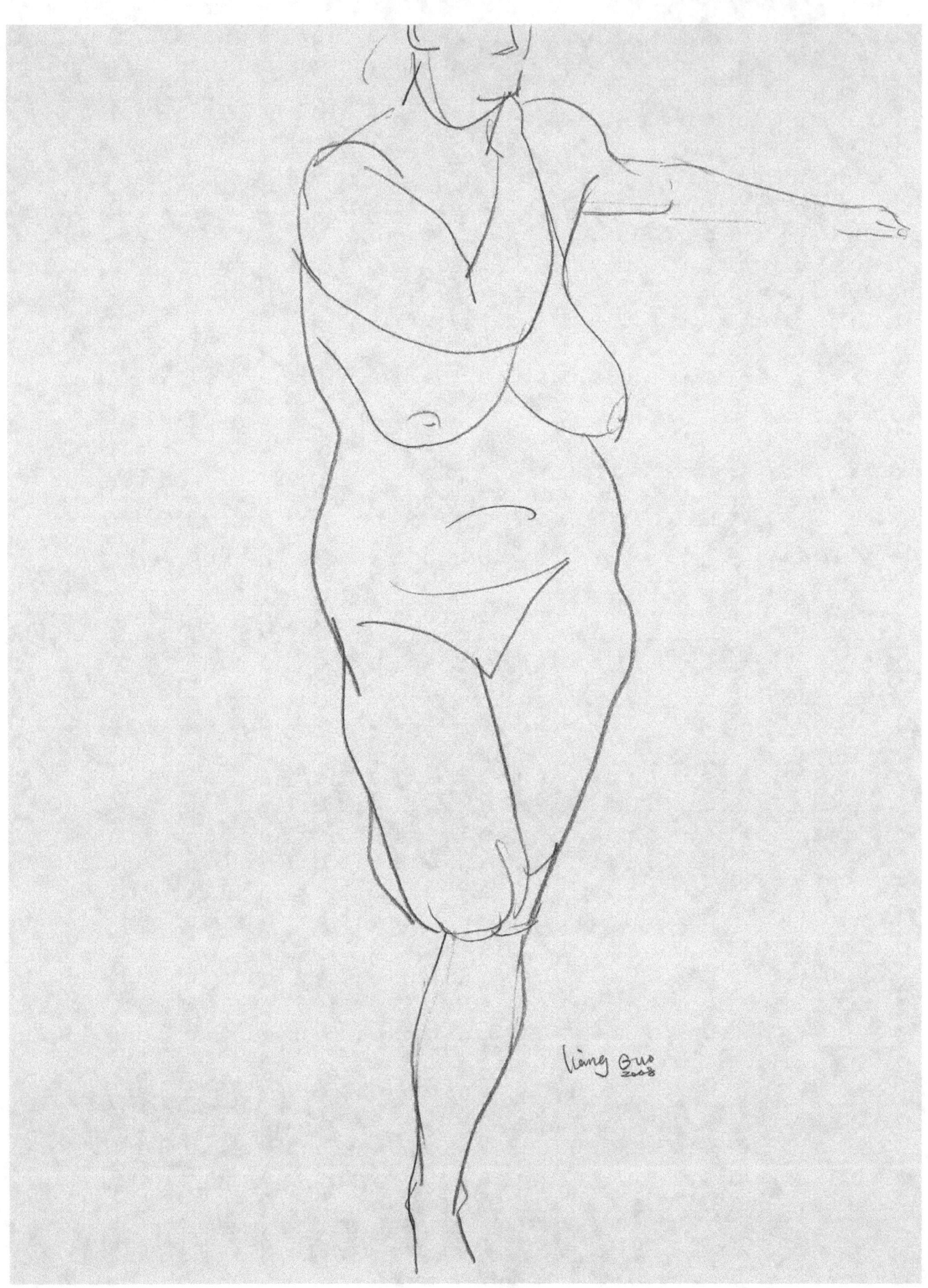

38    Keeping stability, 2008, Pencil

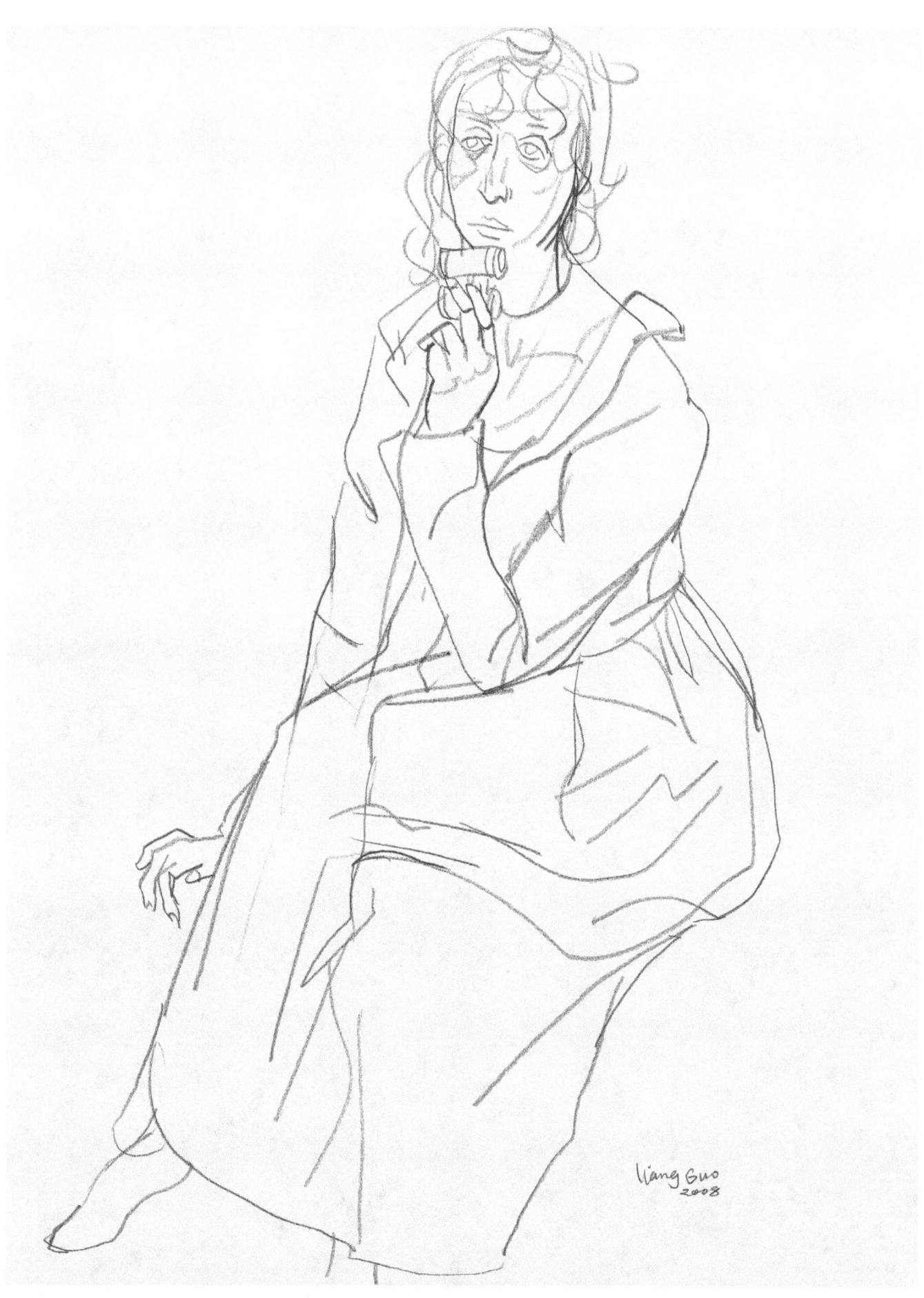

39    Opera glasses, 2008, Pencil

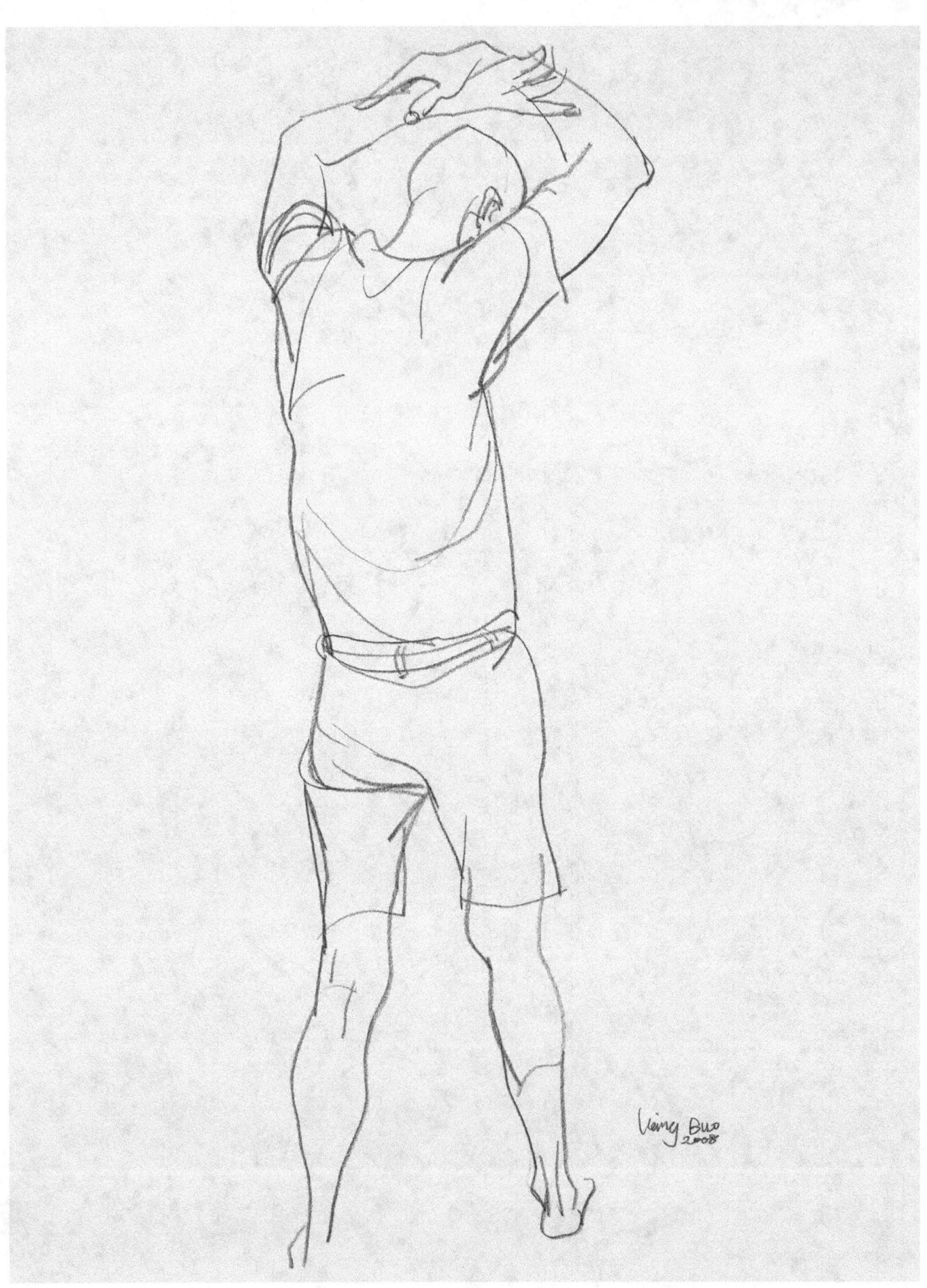

40   Raising the arms, 2008, Pencil

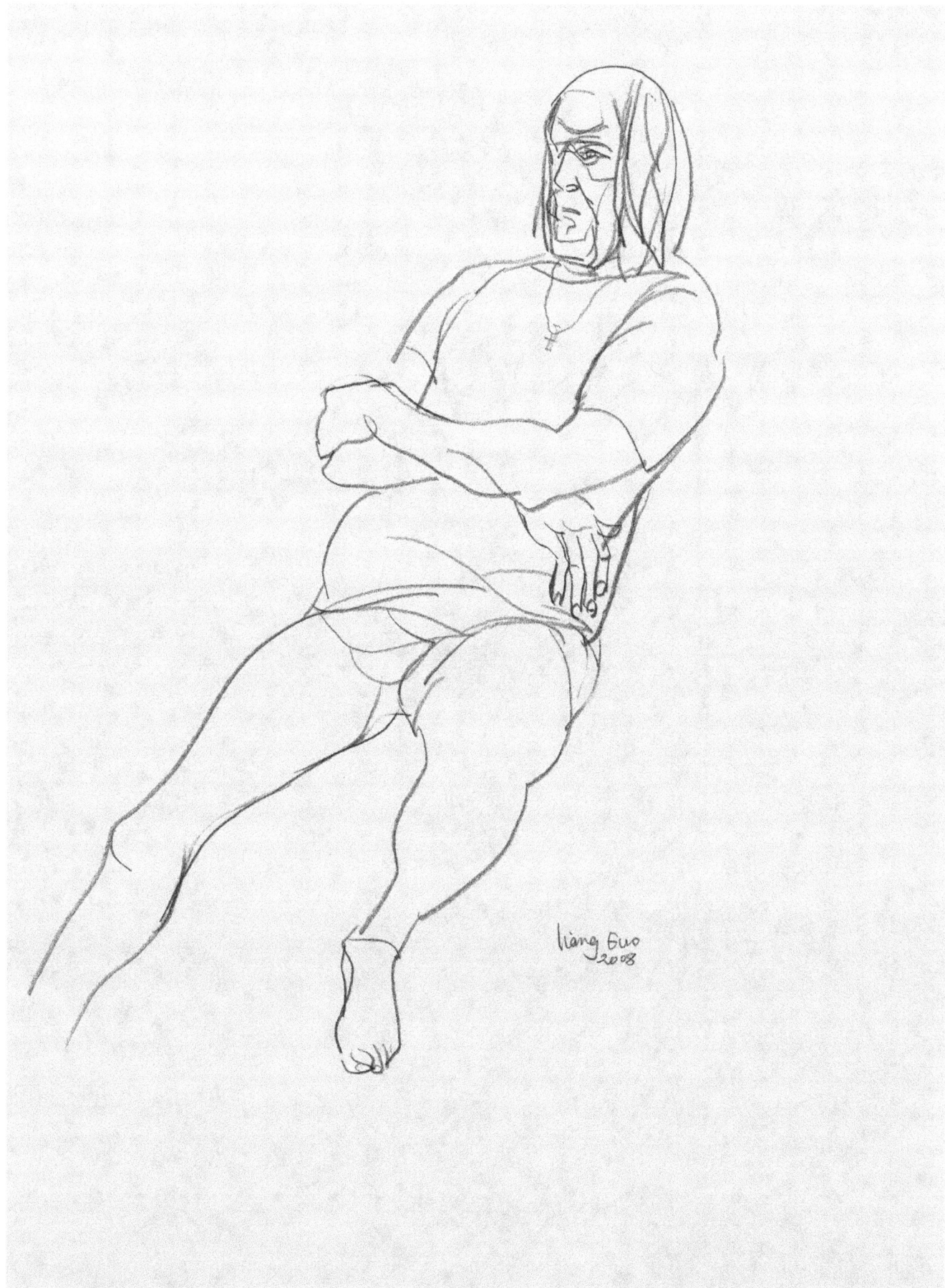

41　Sunny, 2008, Pencil

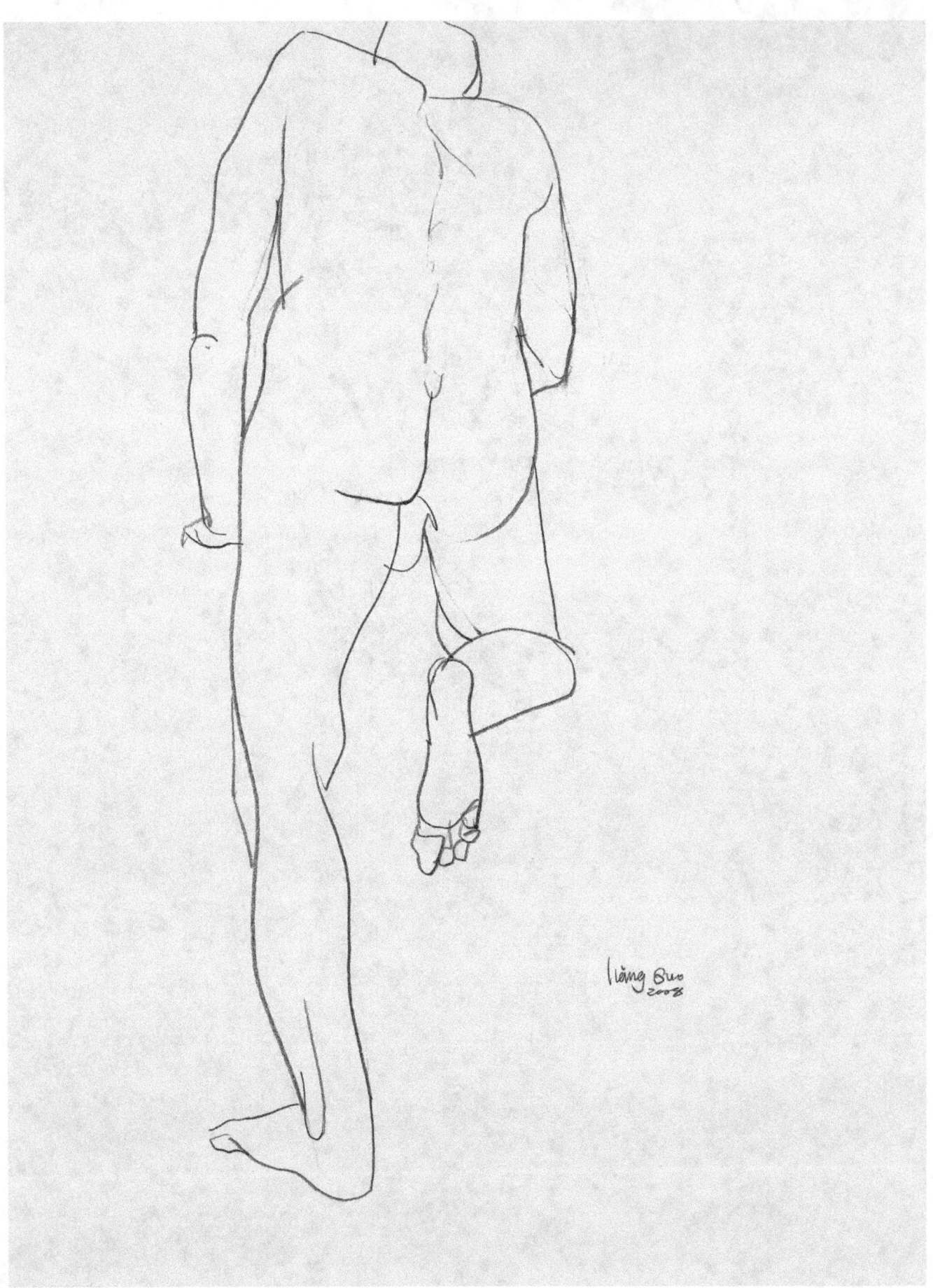

42    Find a way, 2008, Pencil

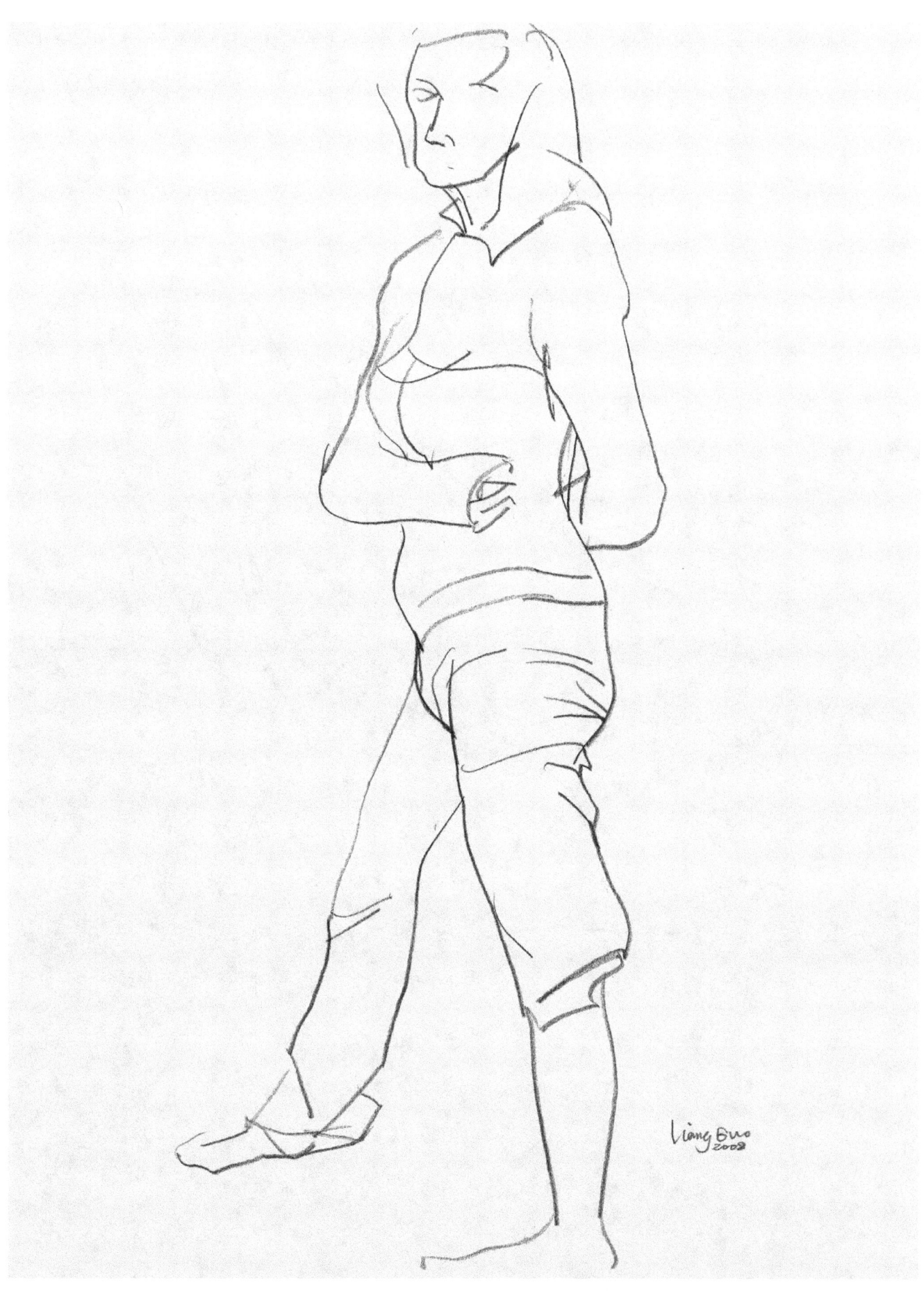

43    Special treat, 2008, Pencil

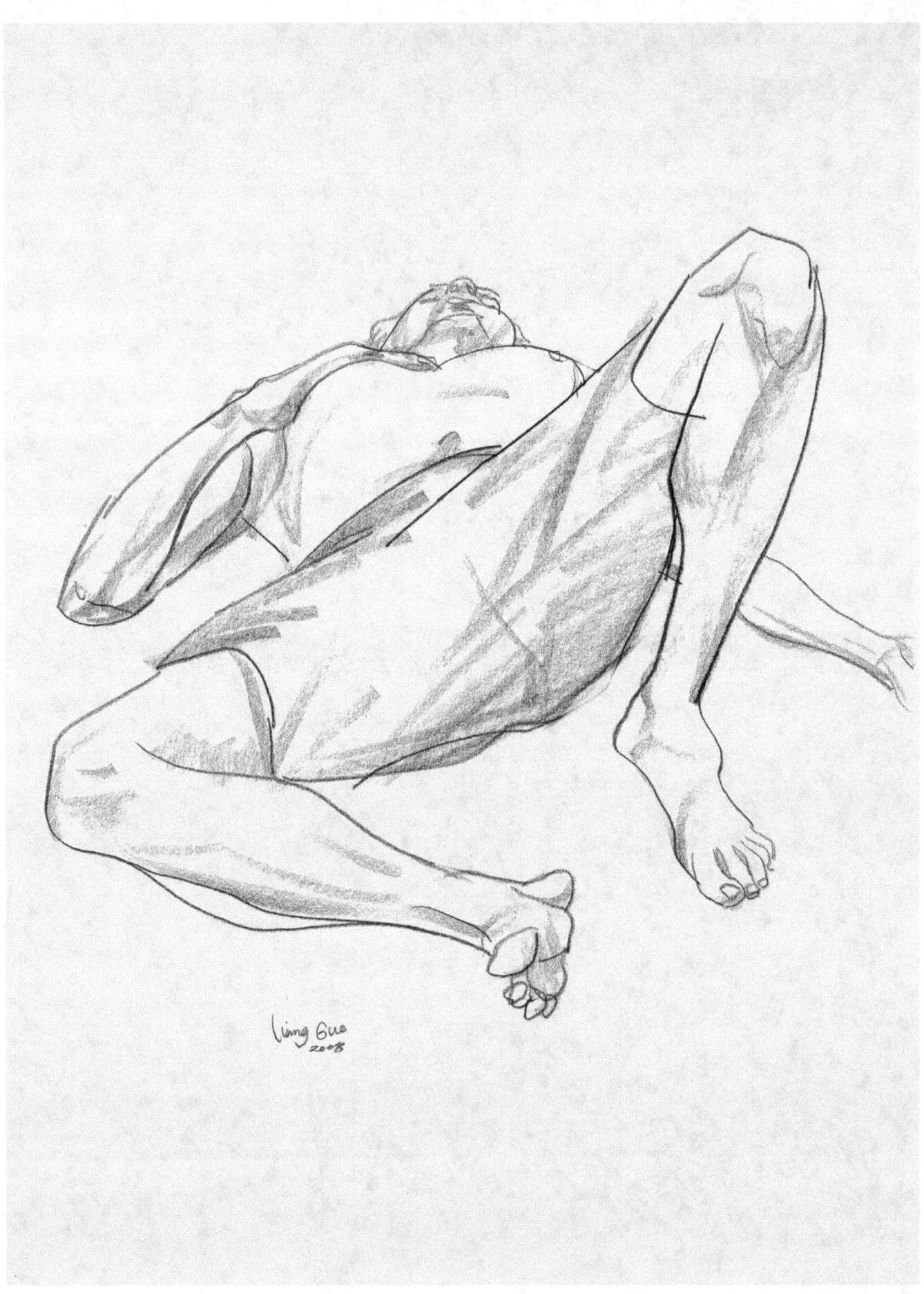

44   Sound sleep, 2008, Monolith pencil

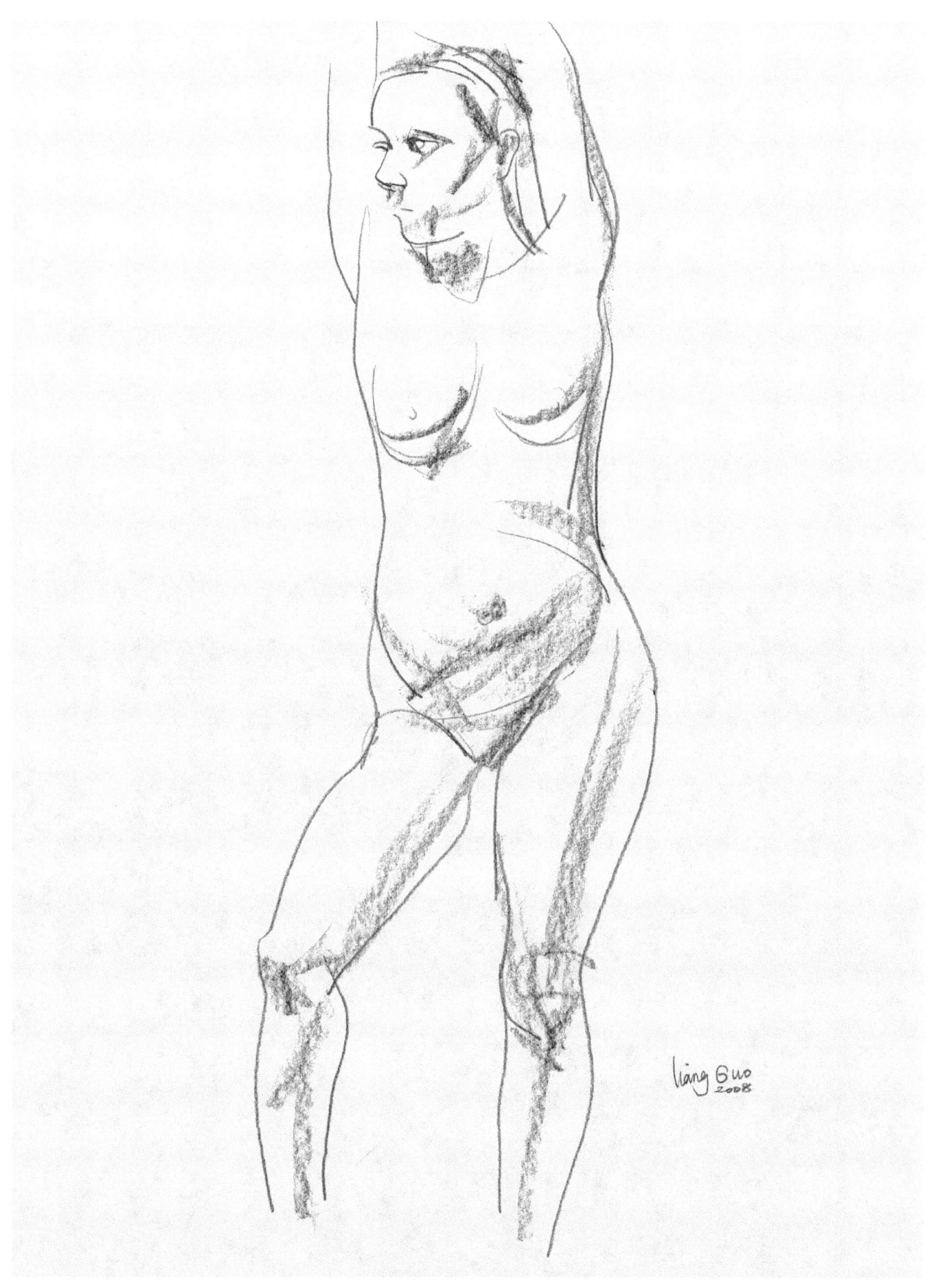

45    Lily, 2008, Charcoal

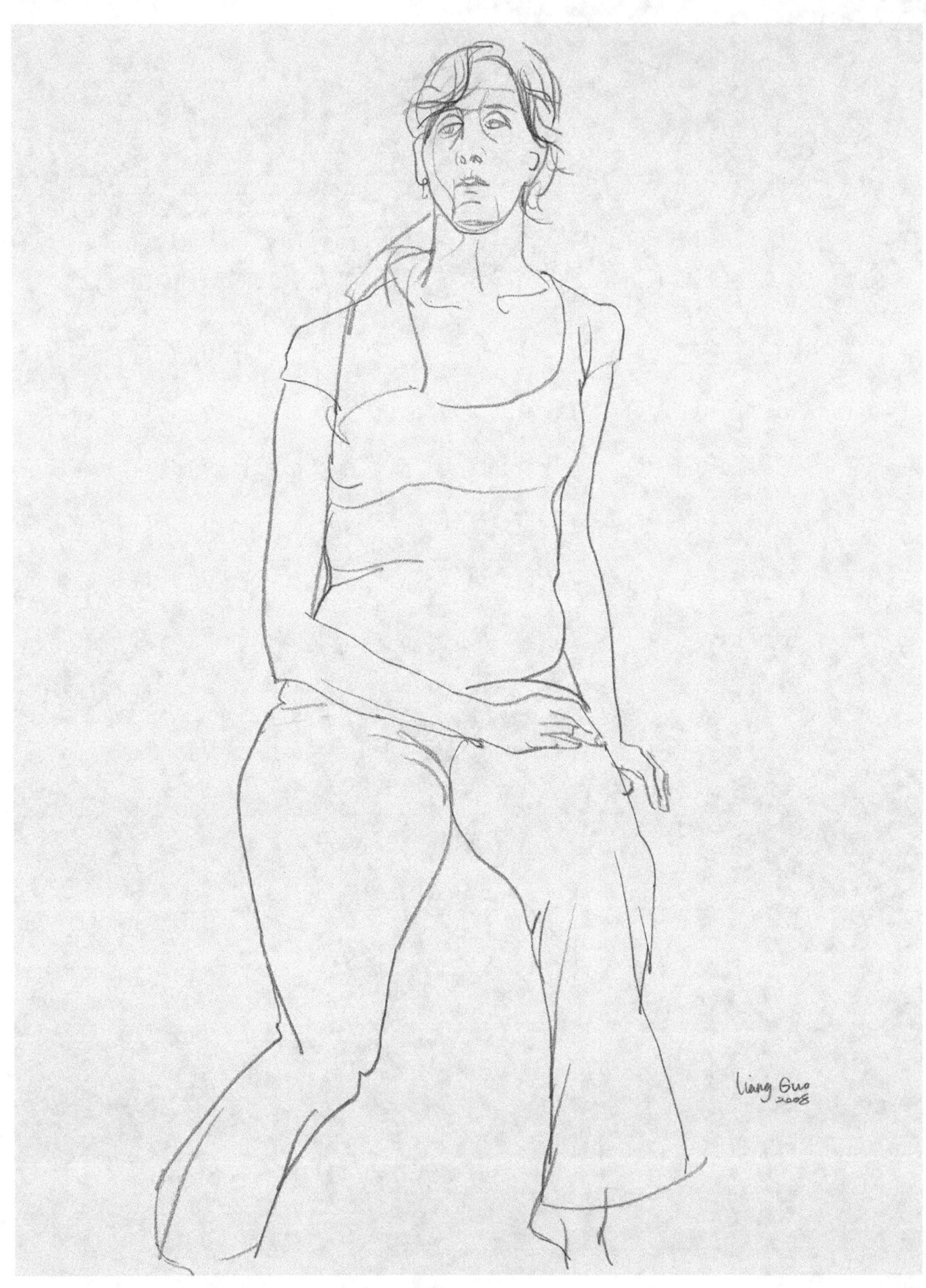

46    Social study, 2008, Pencil

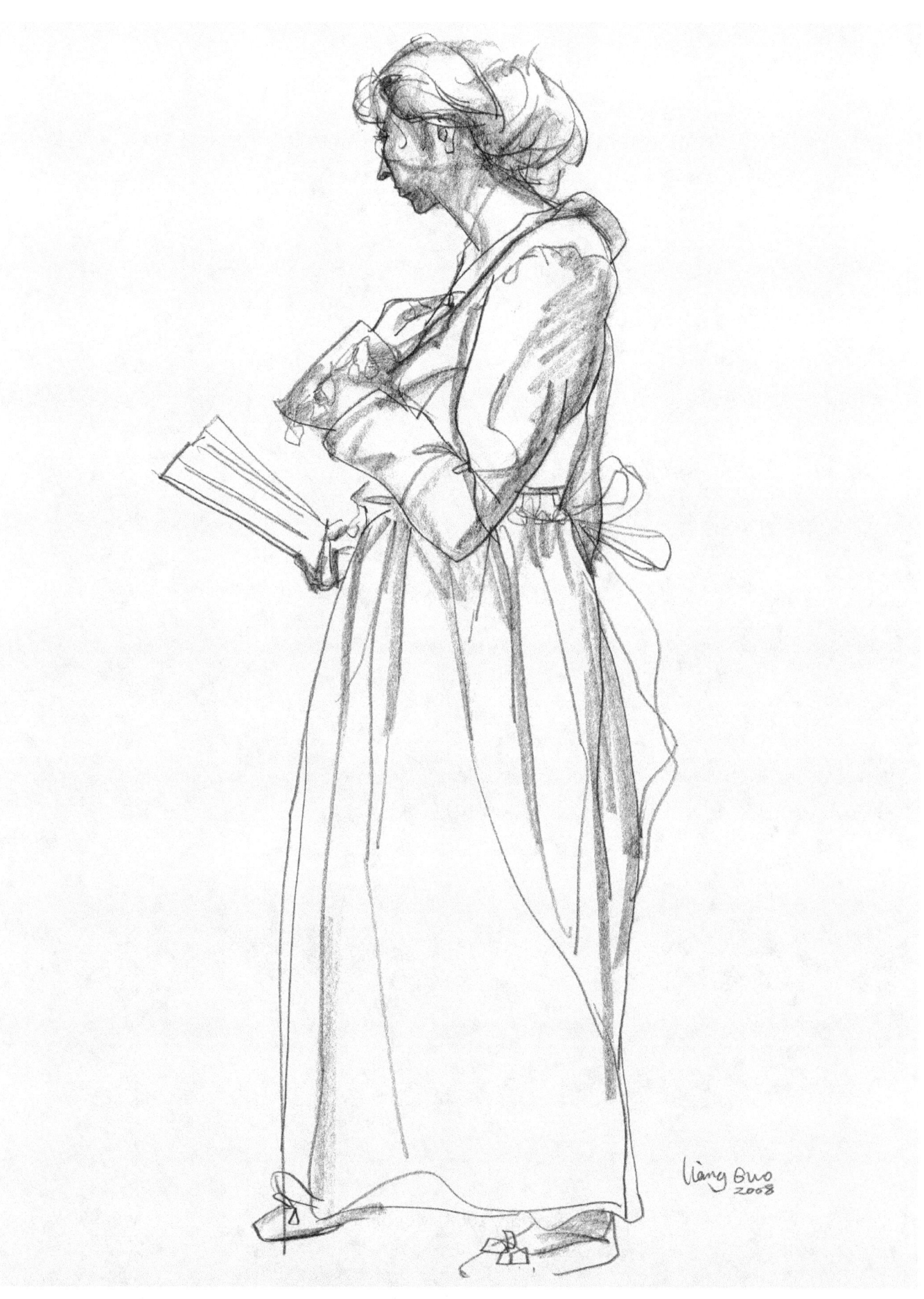

47    Reading, 2008, Pencil and monolith pencil

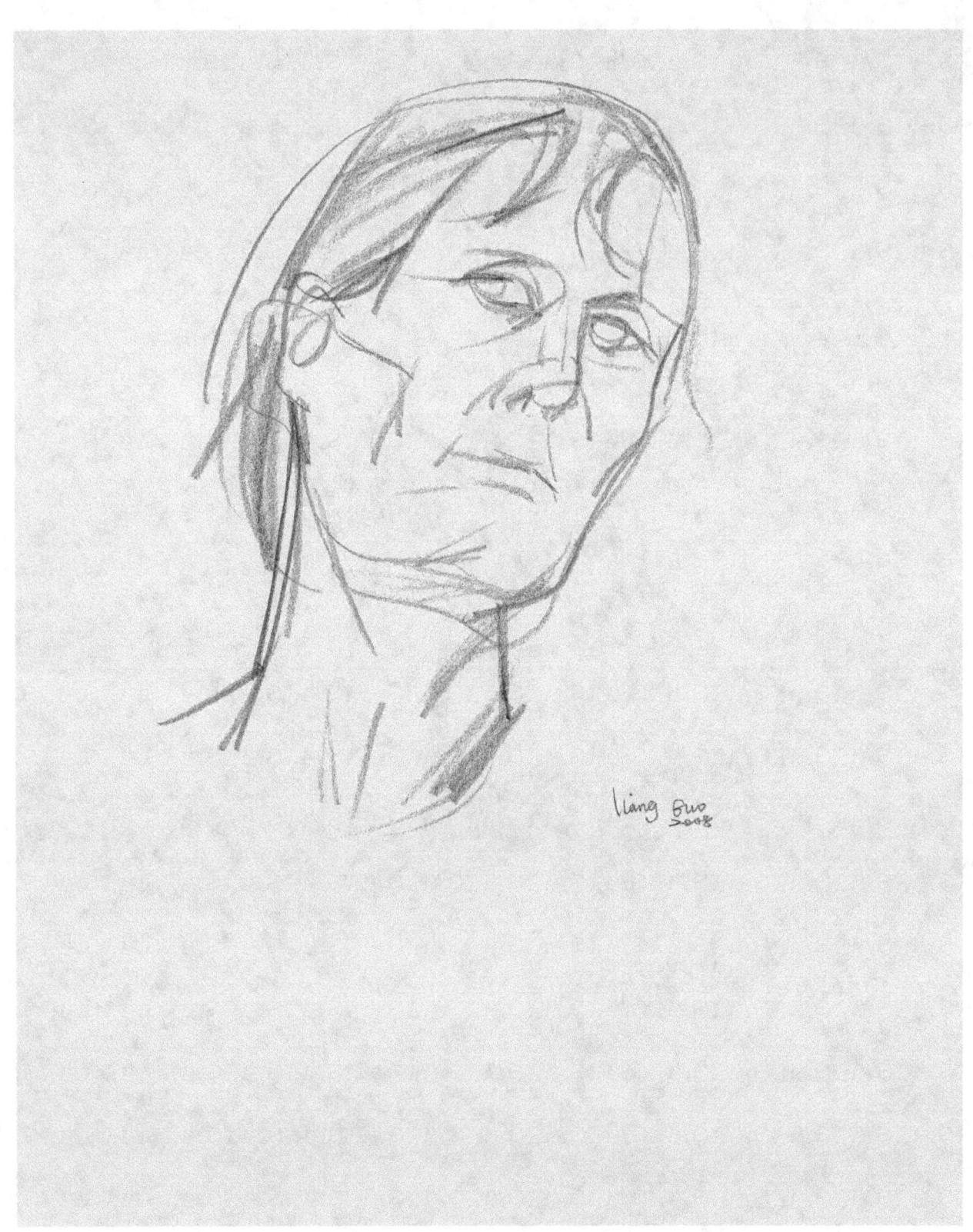

48    Beyond, 2008, Monolith pencil

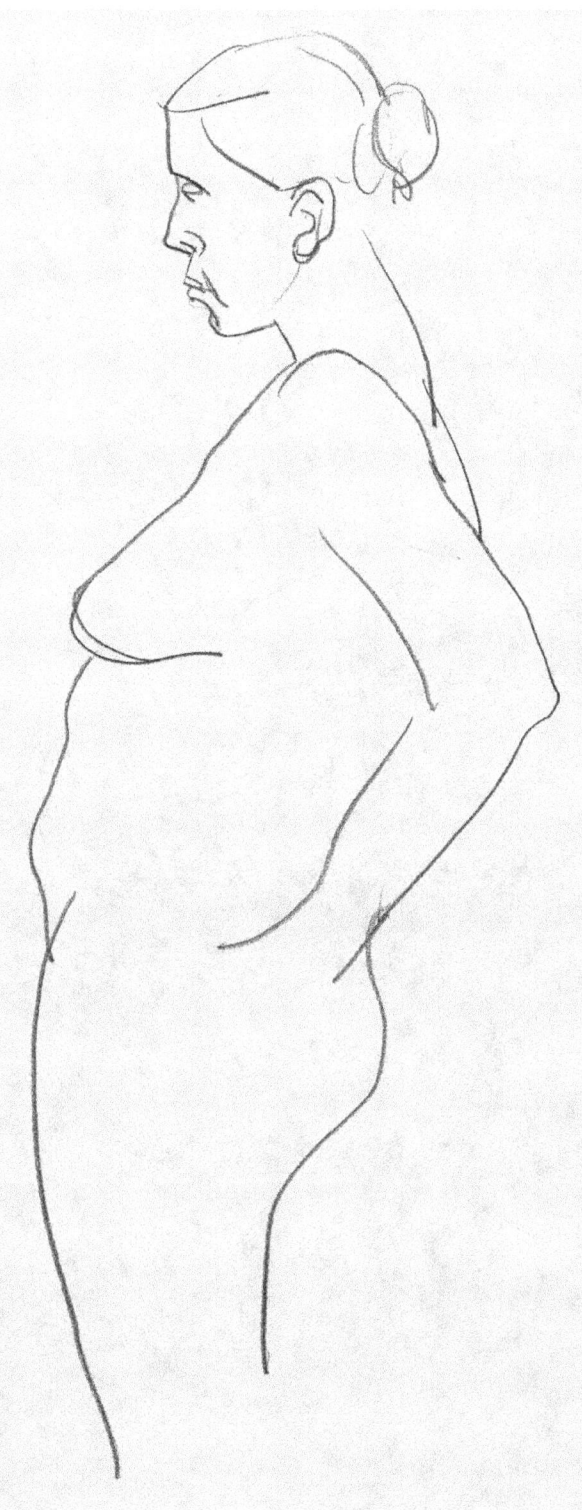

49    Expecting, 2008, Pencil

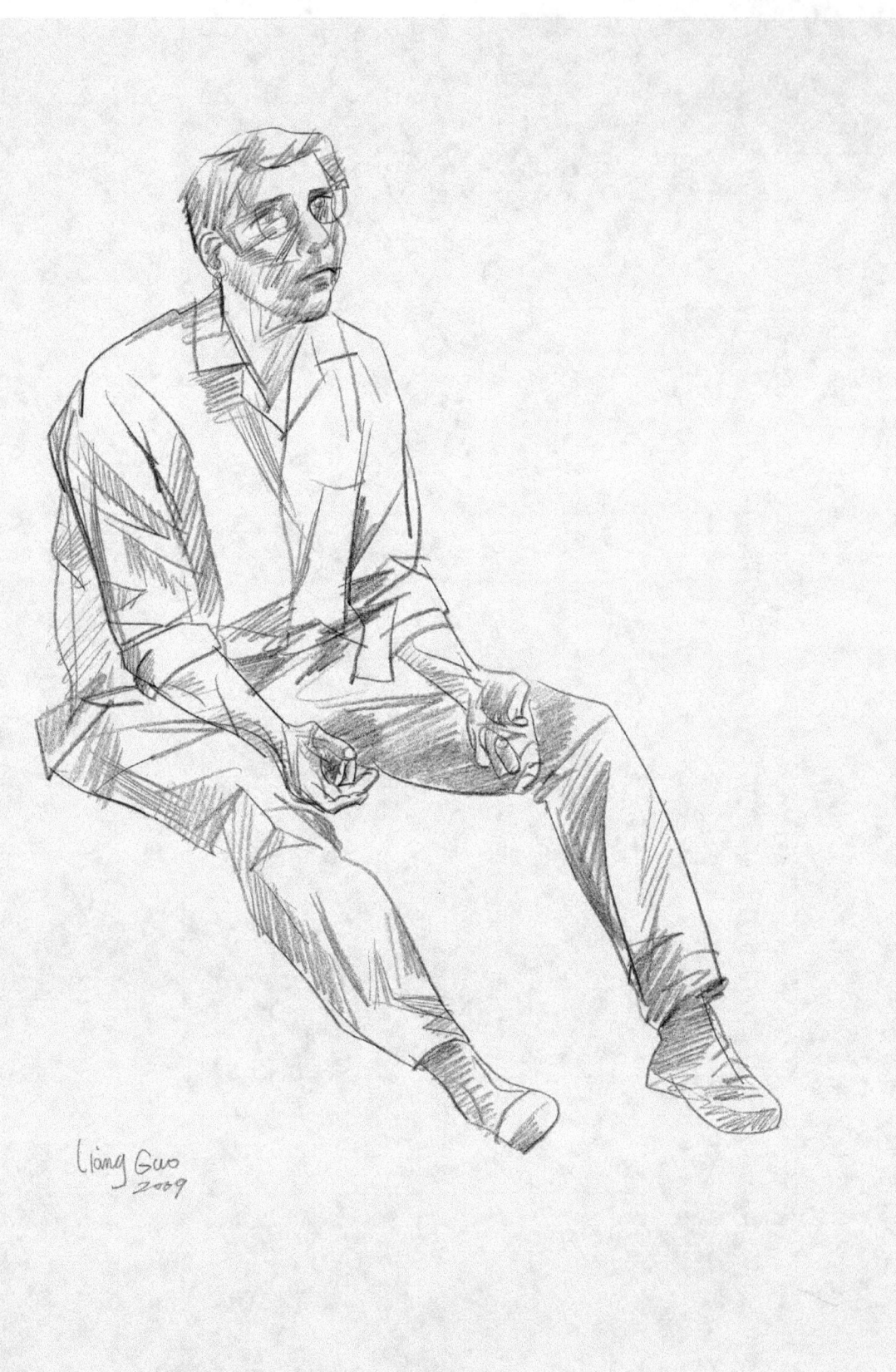

50    Exhausted, 2009, Pencil

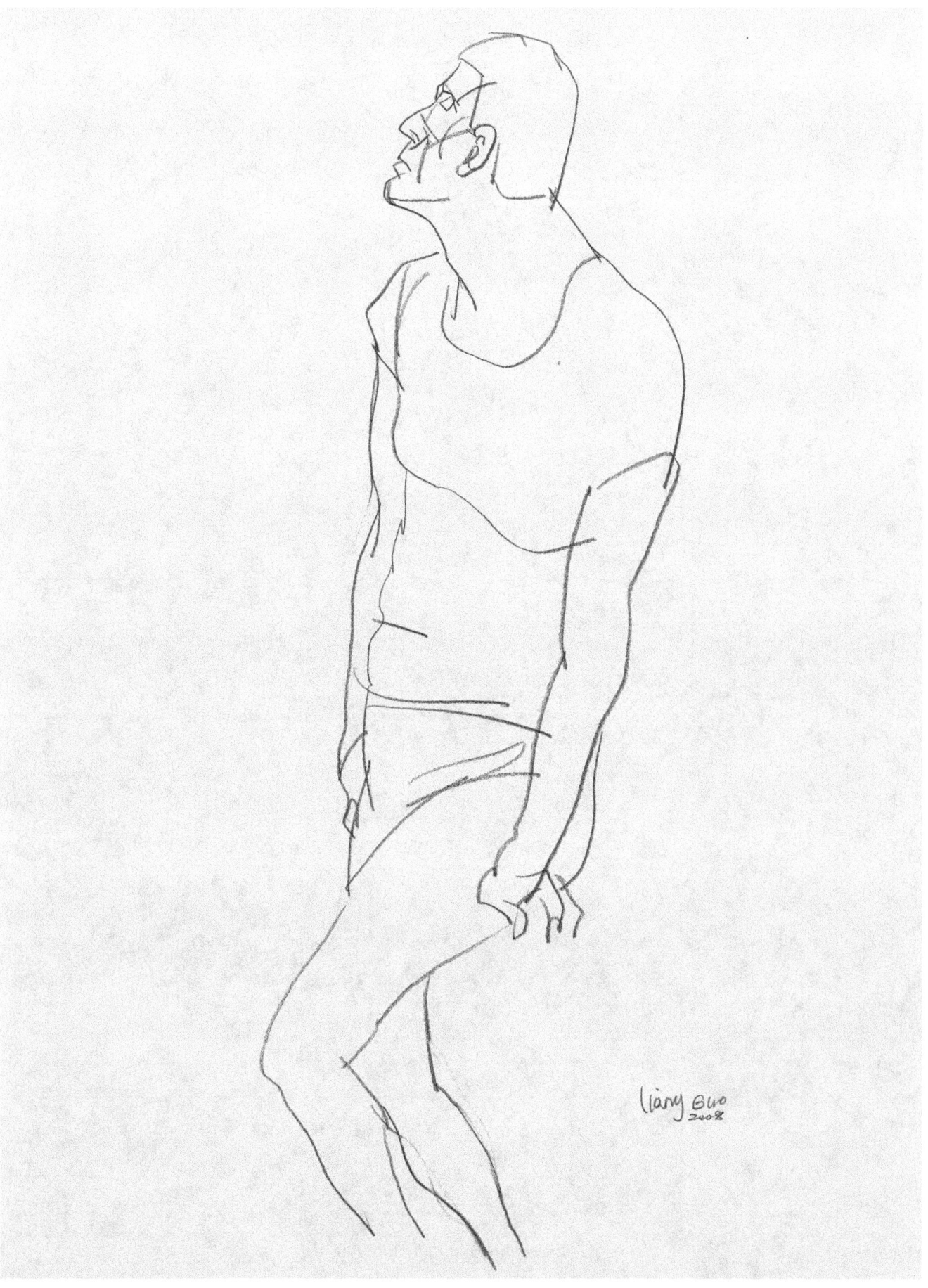

51    Hurry up, 2008, Pencil

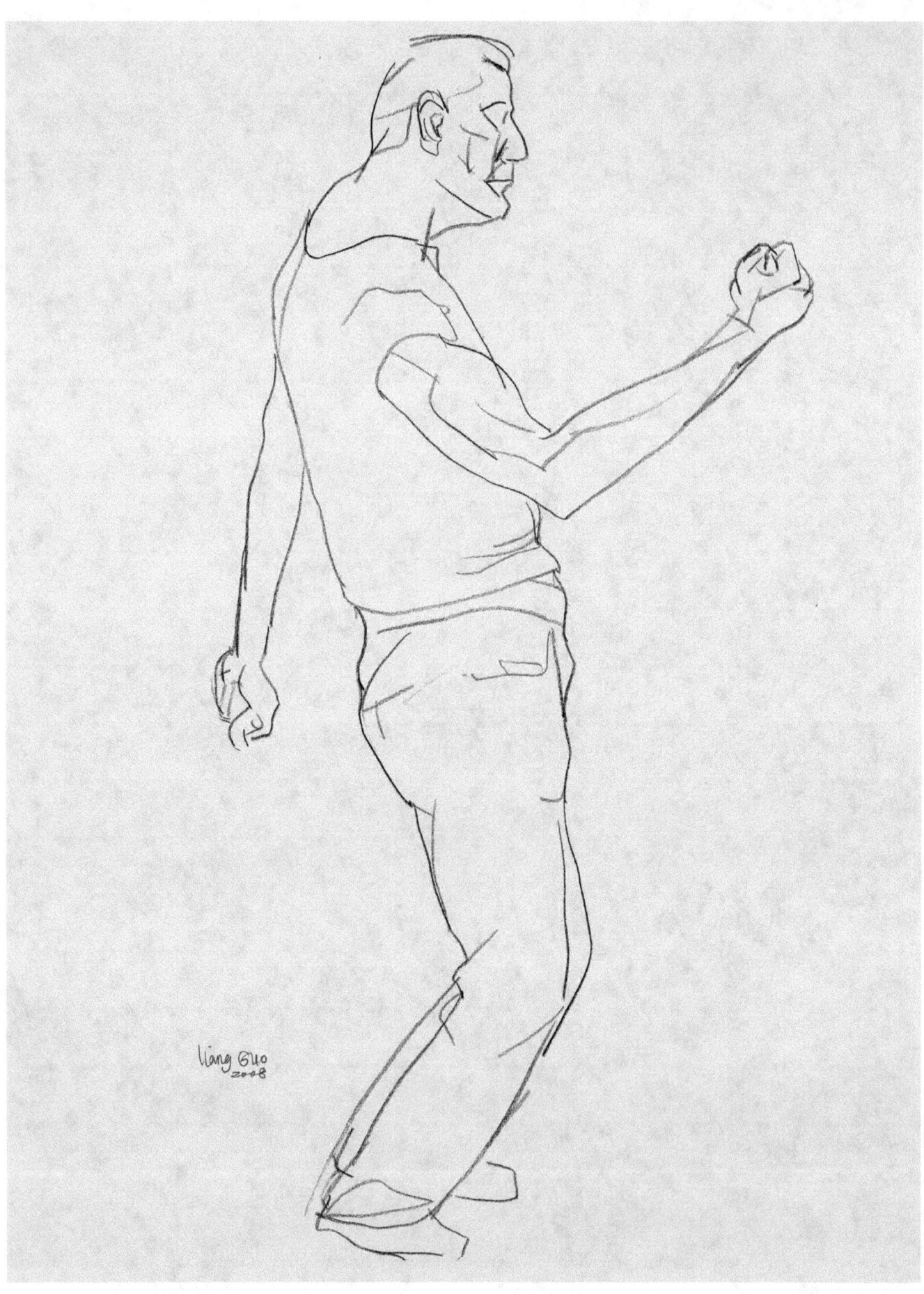

52    For sure, 2008, Pencil

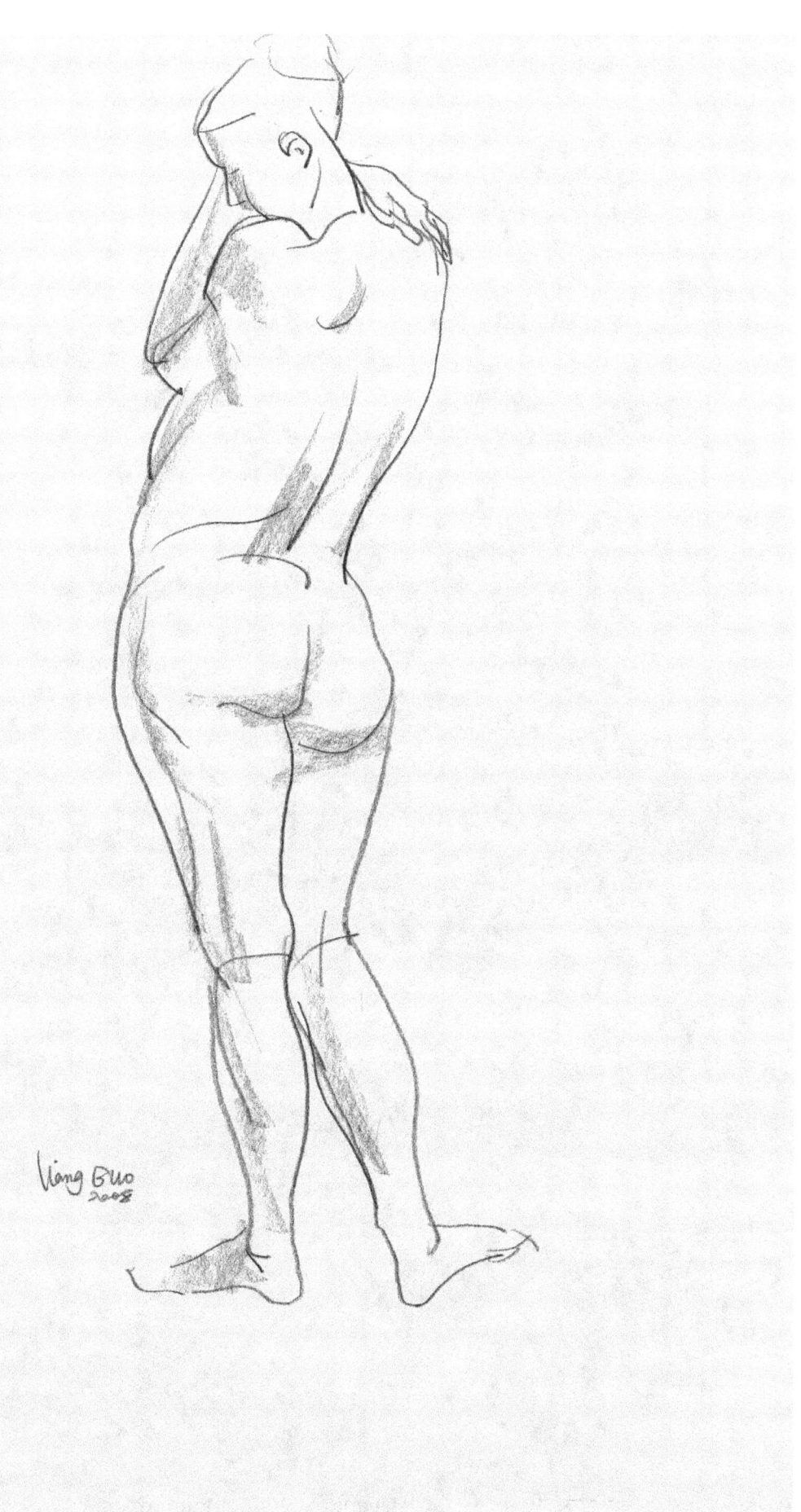

53    Back, 2008, Monolith pencil

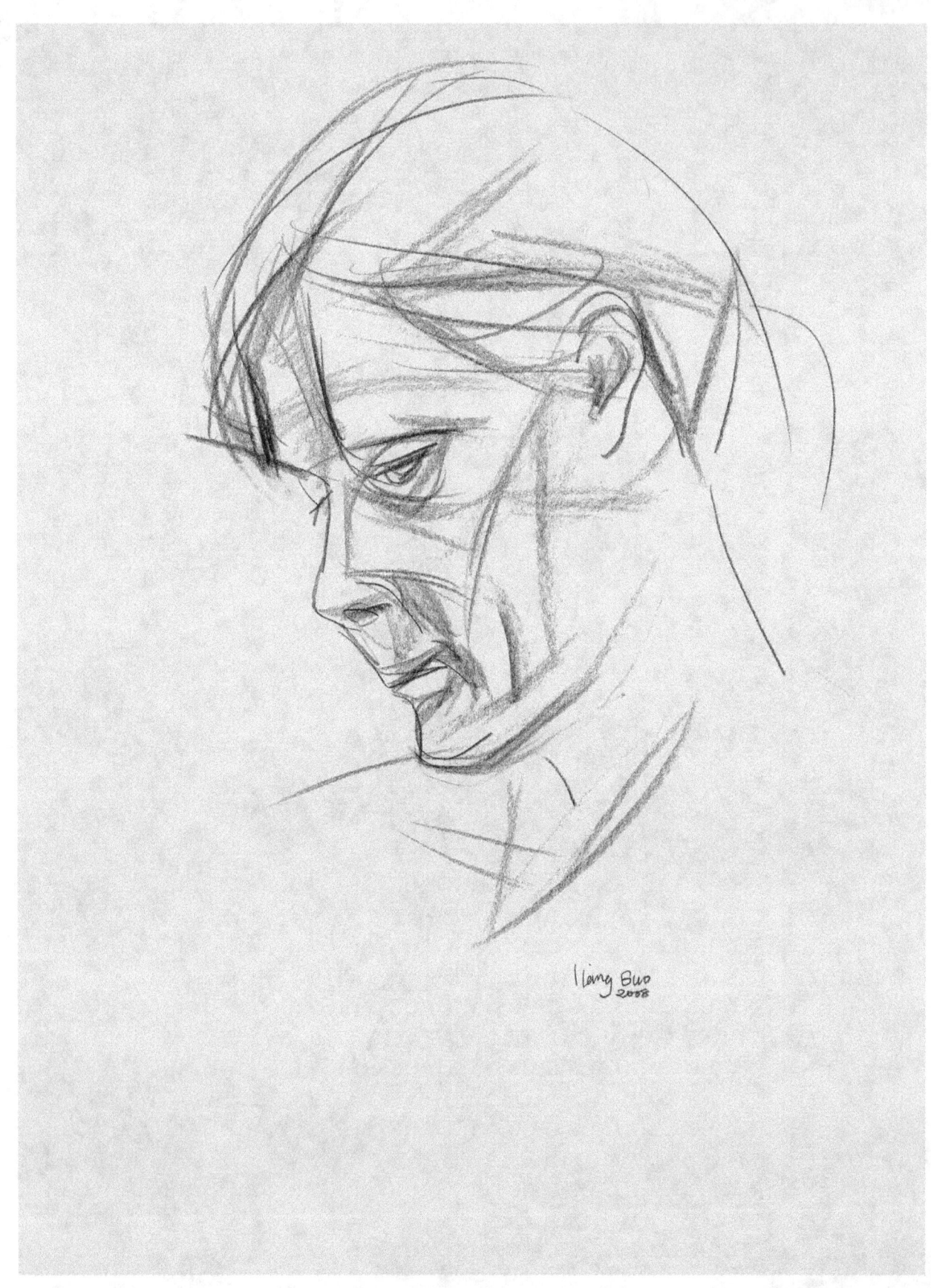

54    Overlook, 2008, Monolith pencil

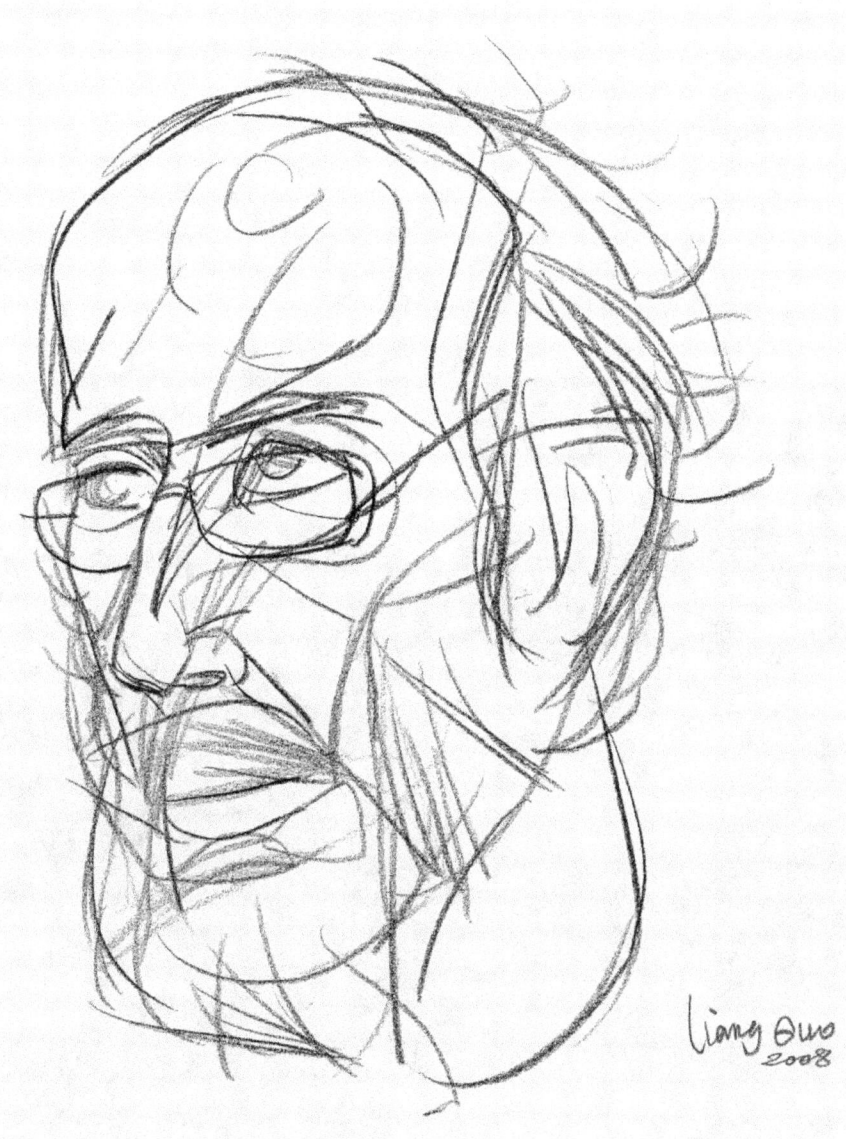

55    Bi-focal, 2008, Charcoal

56   Dancer, 2009, Monolith pencil

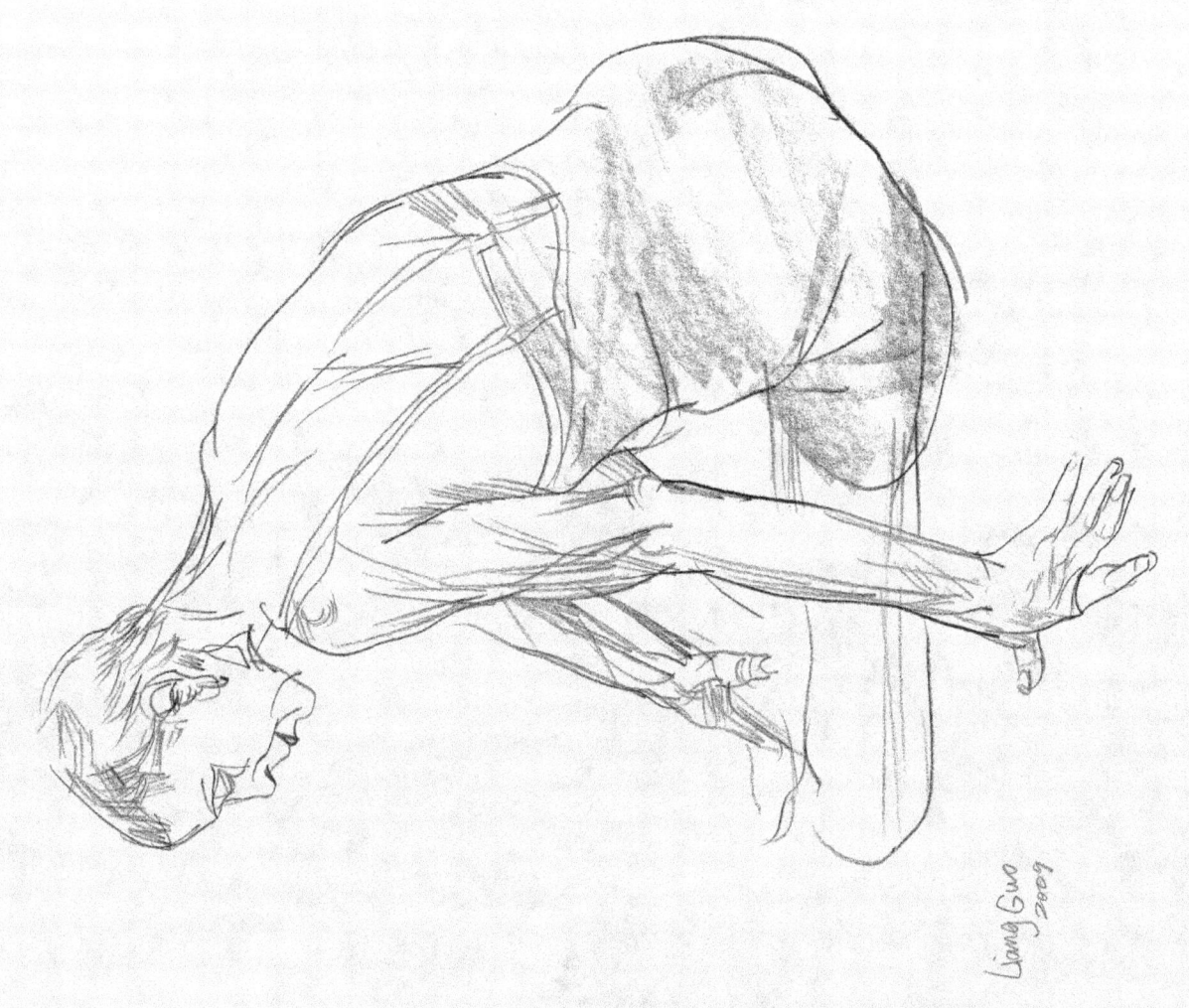

57    Tangram, 2009, Pencil and charcoal

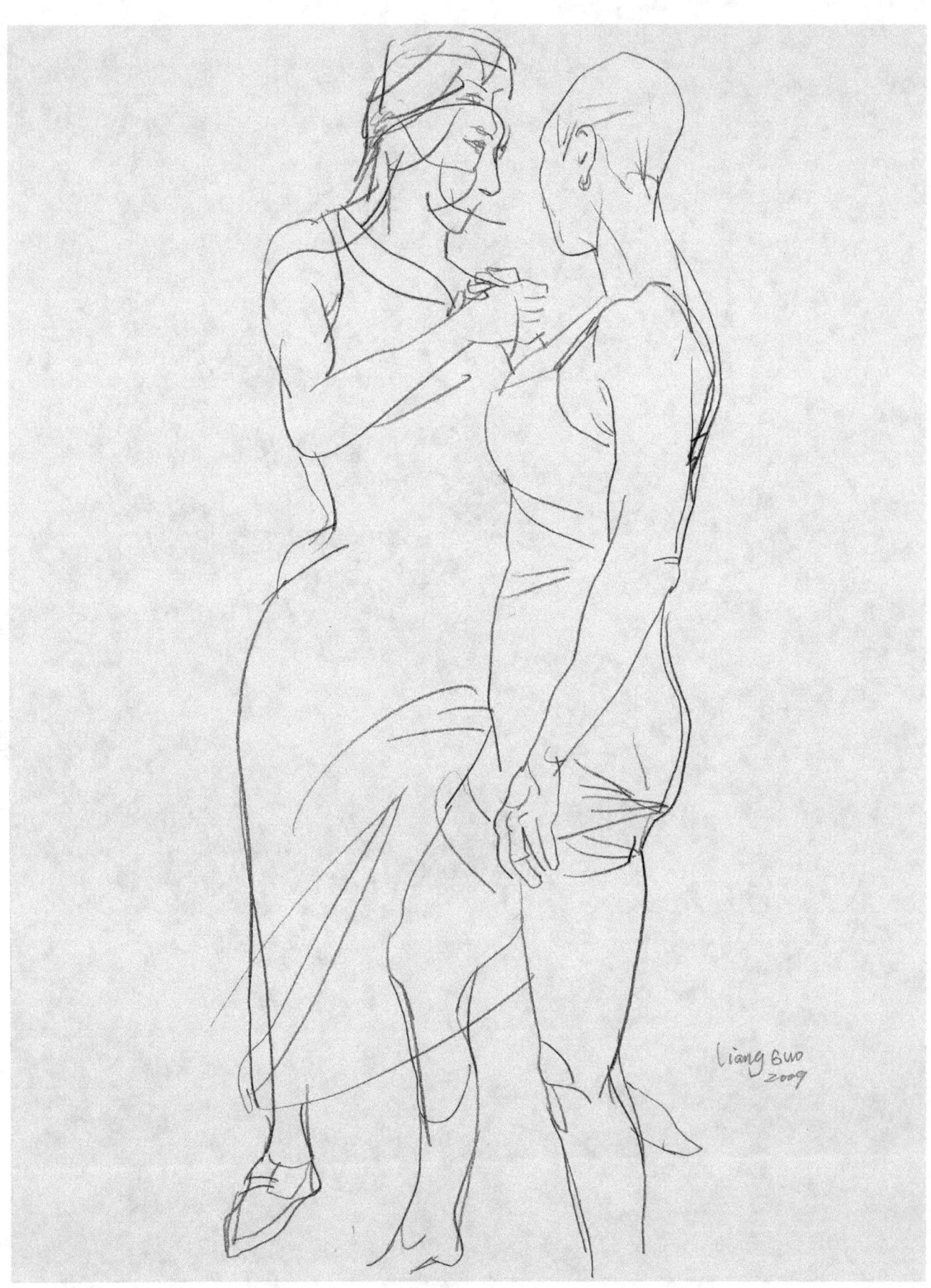

58    Progressive, 2009, Pencil

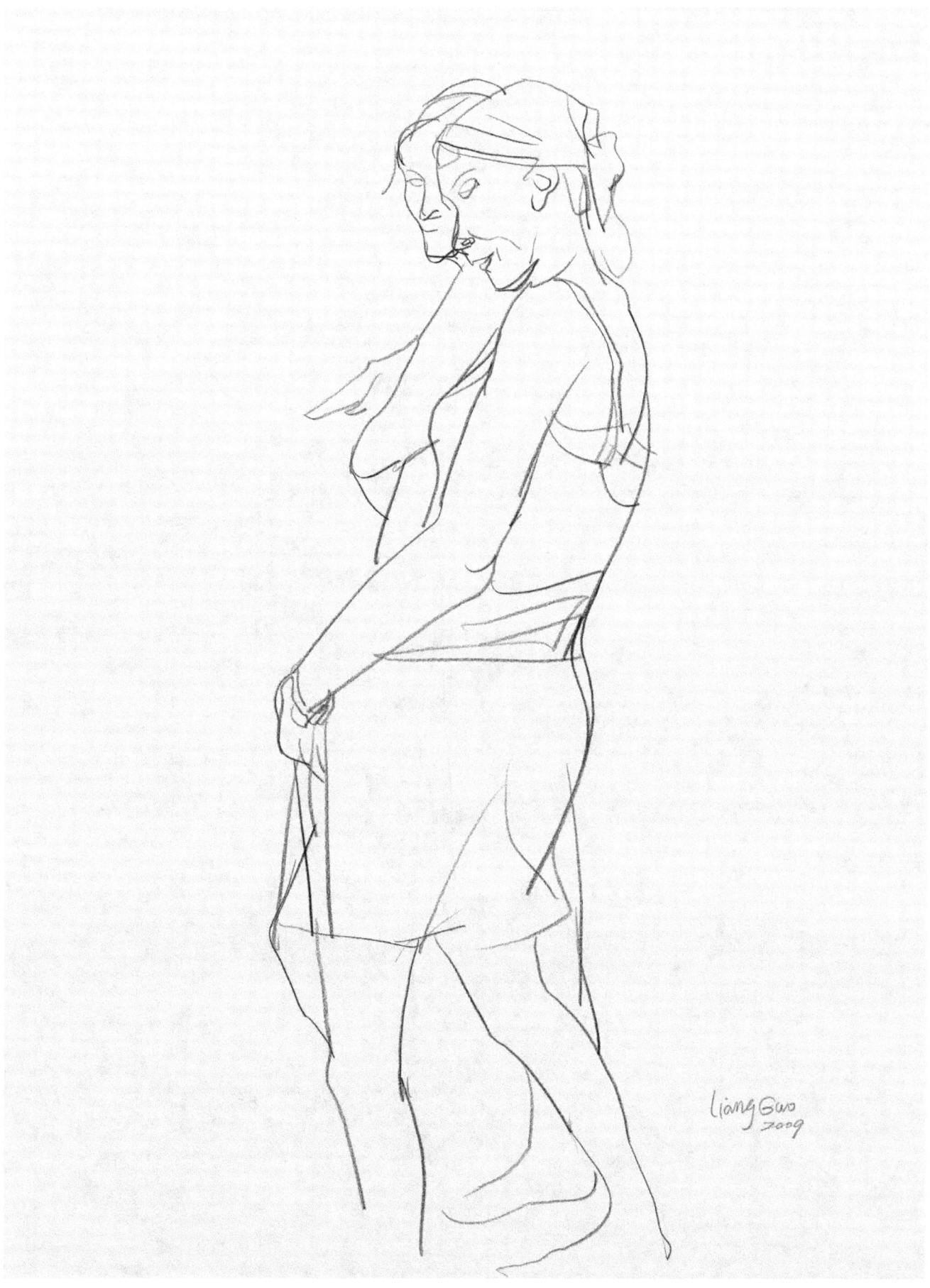

59    Side by side, 2009, Charcoal

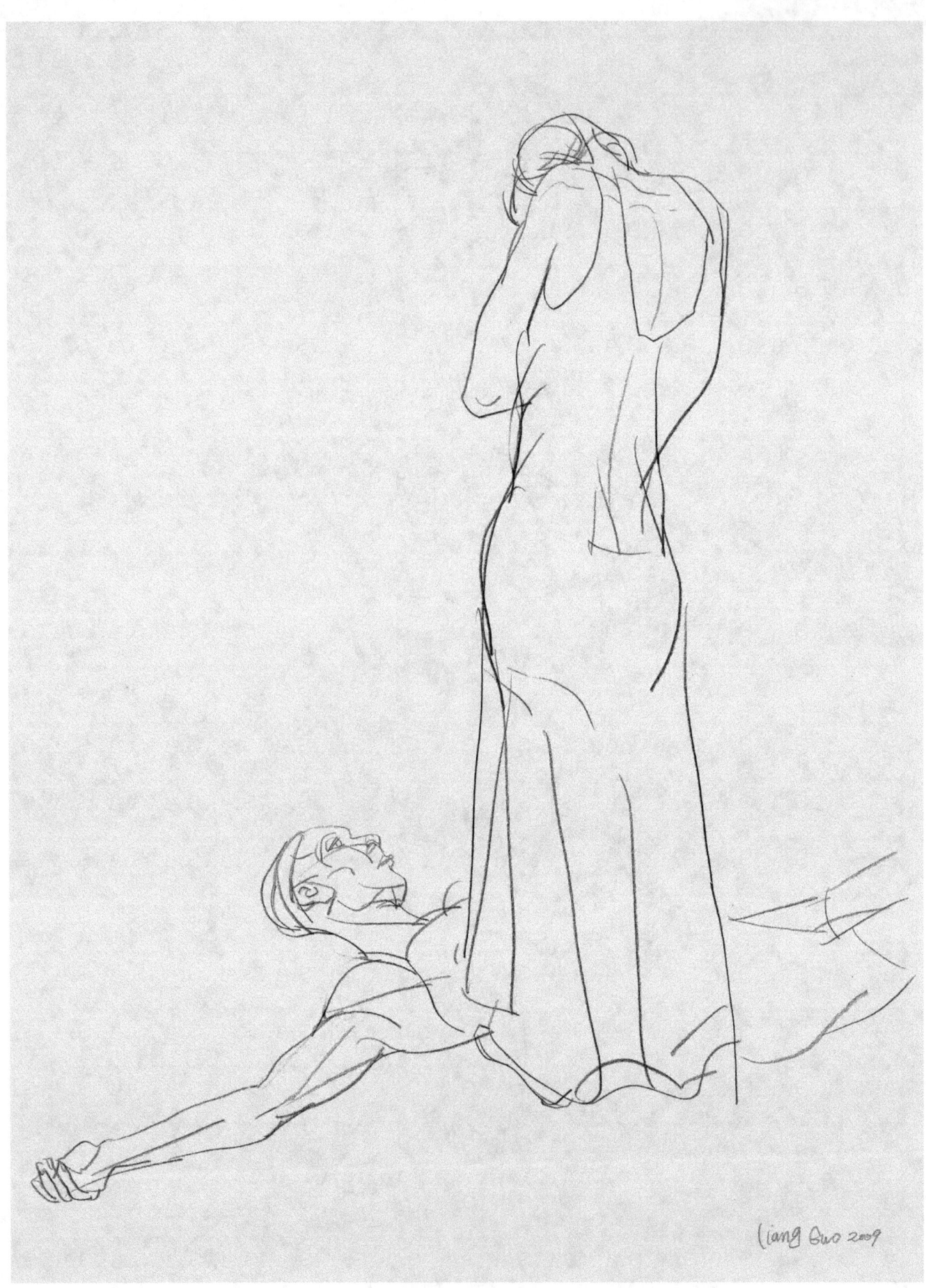

60    Blessing, 2009, Pencil

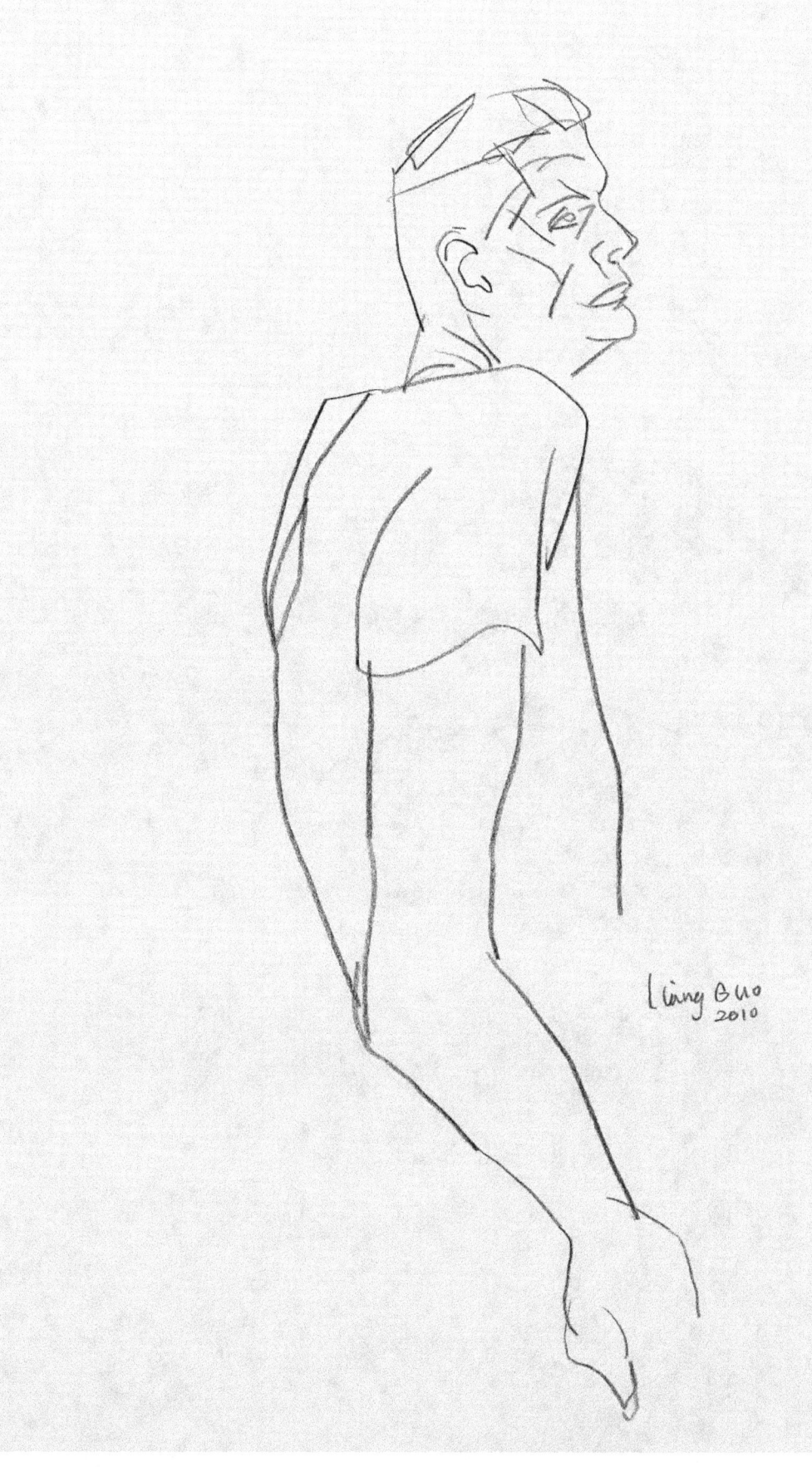

61    The passion of, 2010, Pencil

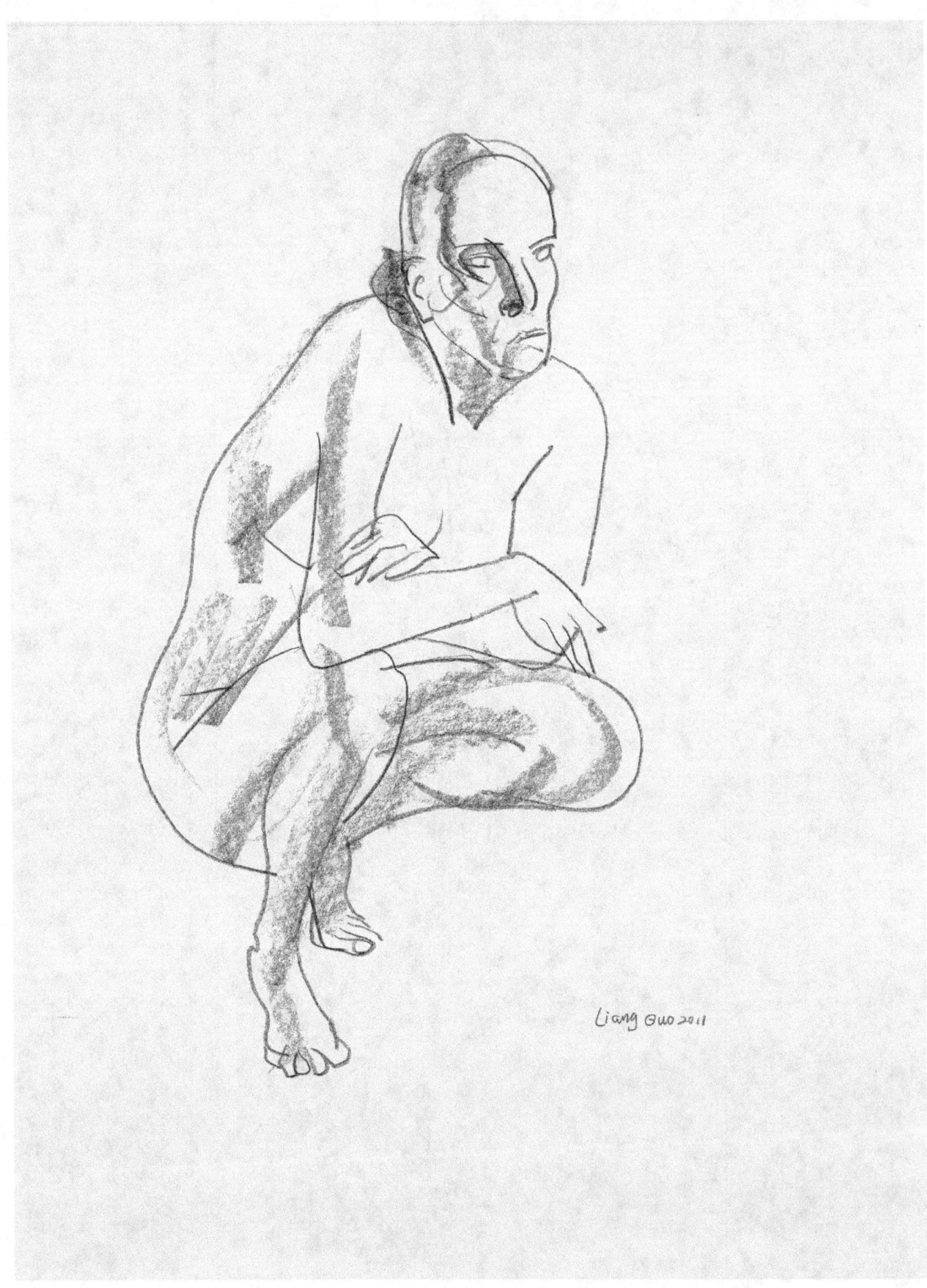

62    Who am I looking for, 2011, Pencil and charcoal

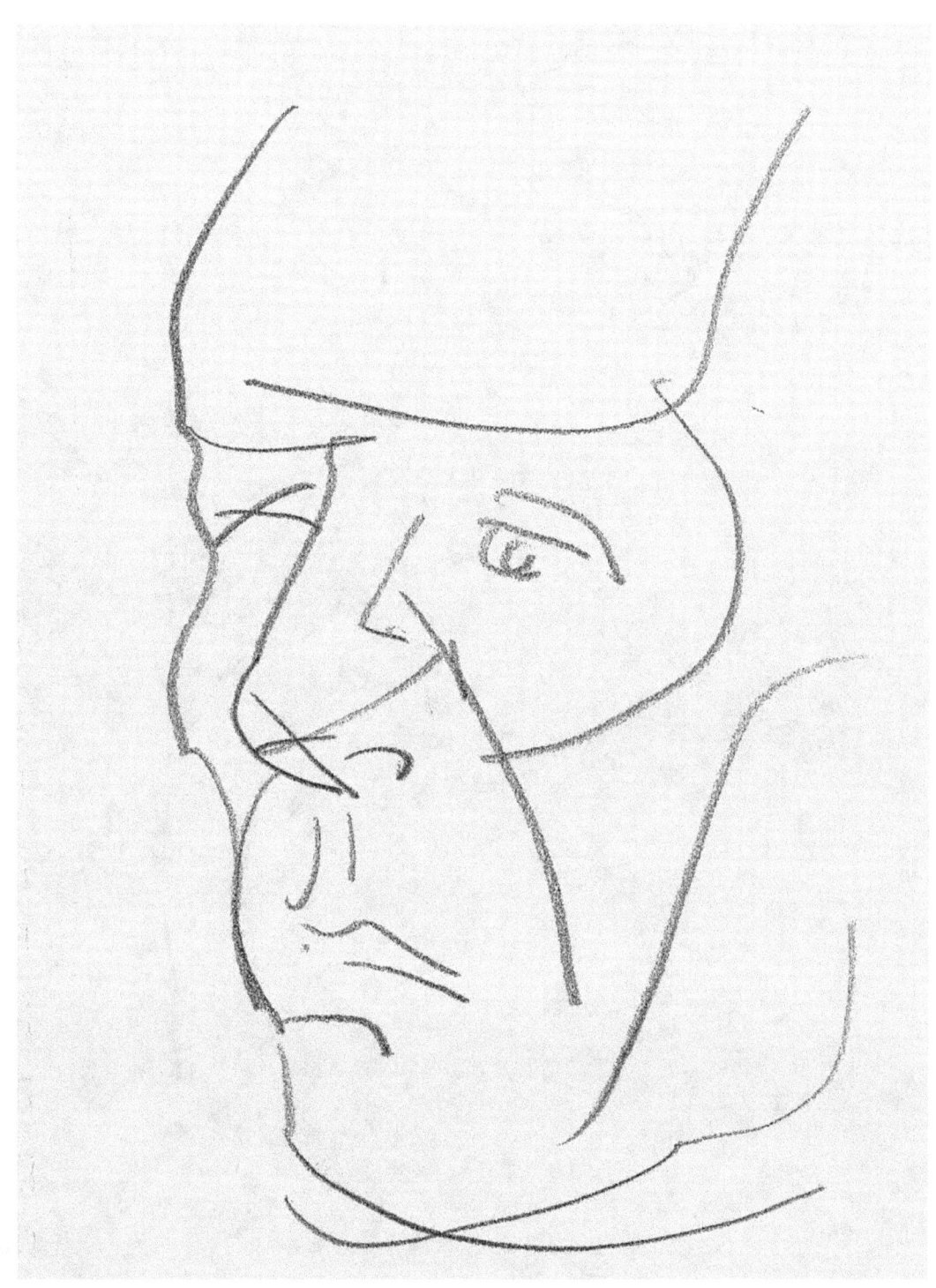

63    A melancholic man, 2011, Pencil

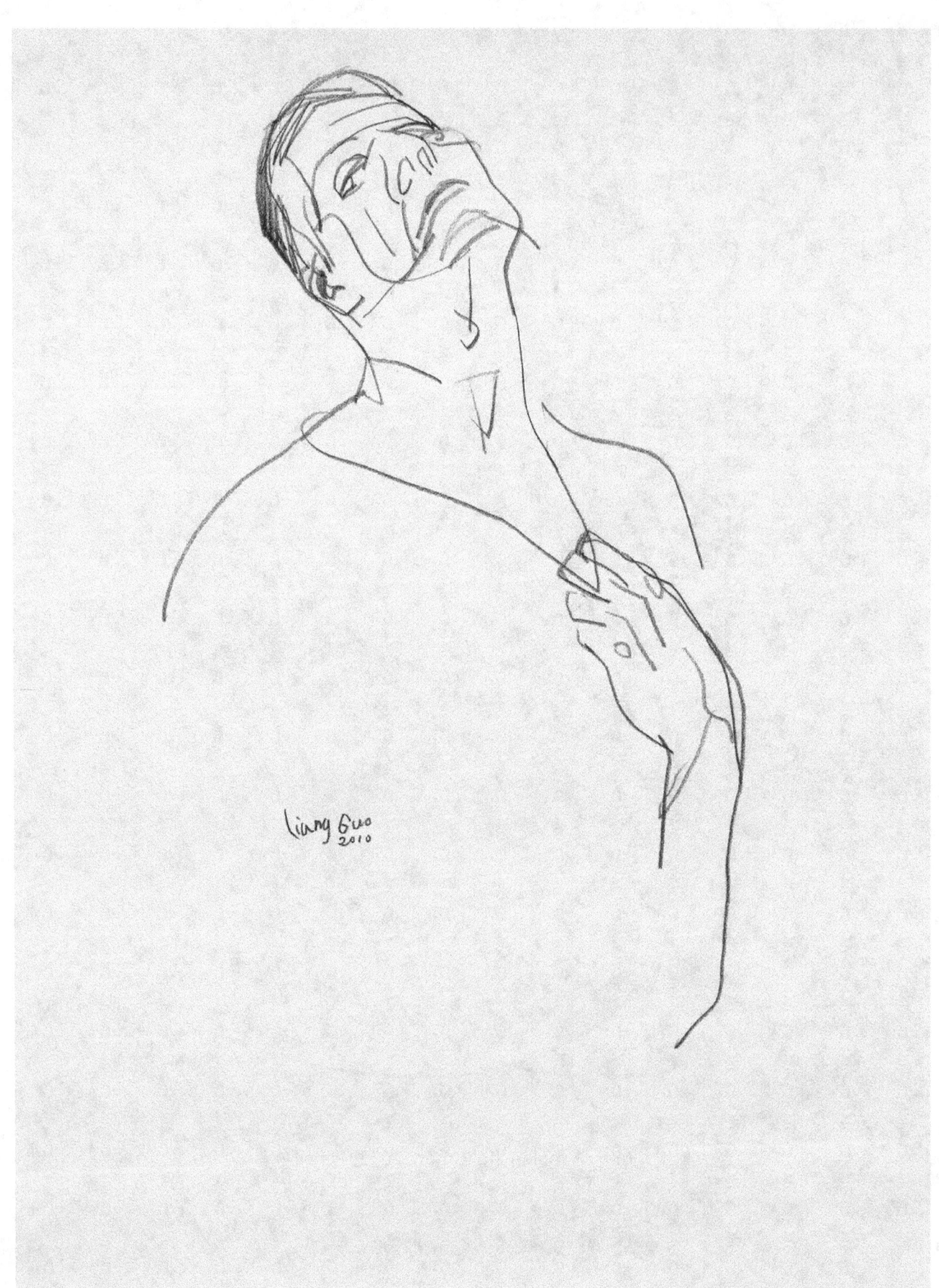

64    Craze, 2010, Pencil

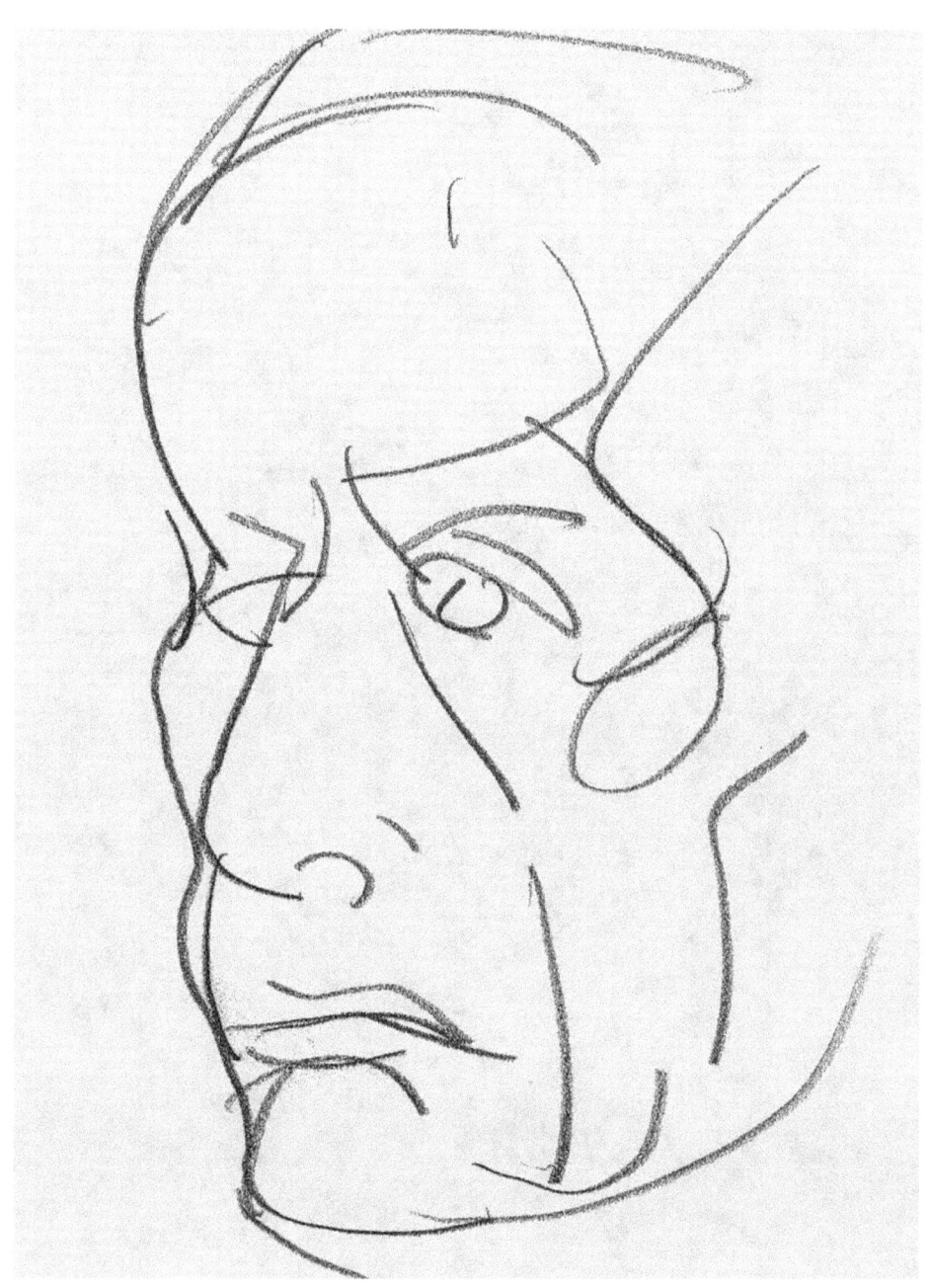

65    Whatever, 2011, Pencil

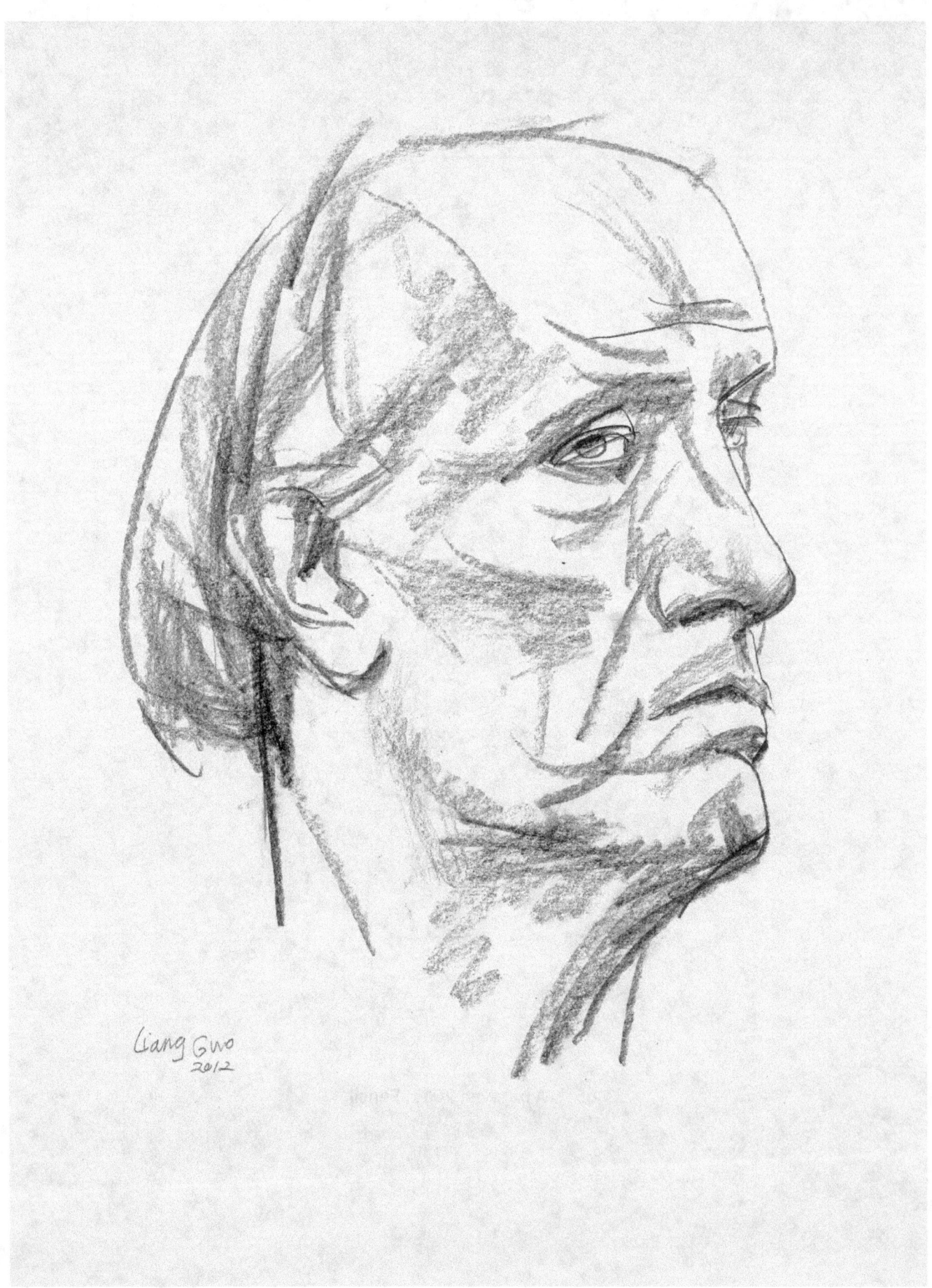

66    At loss, 2012, Monolith pencil

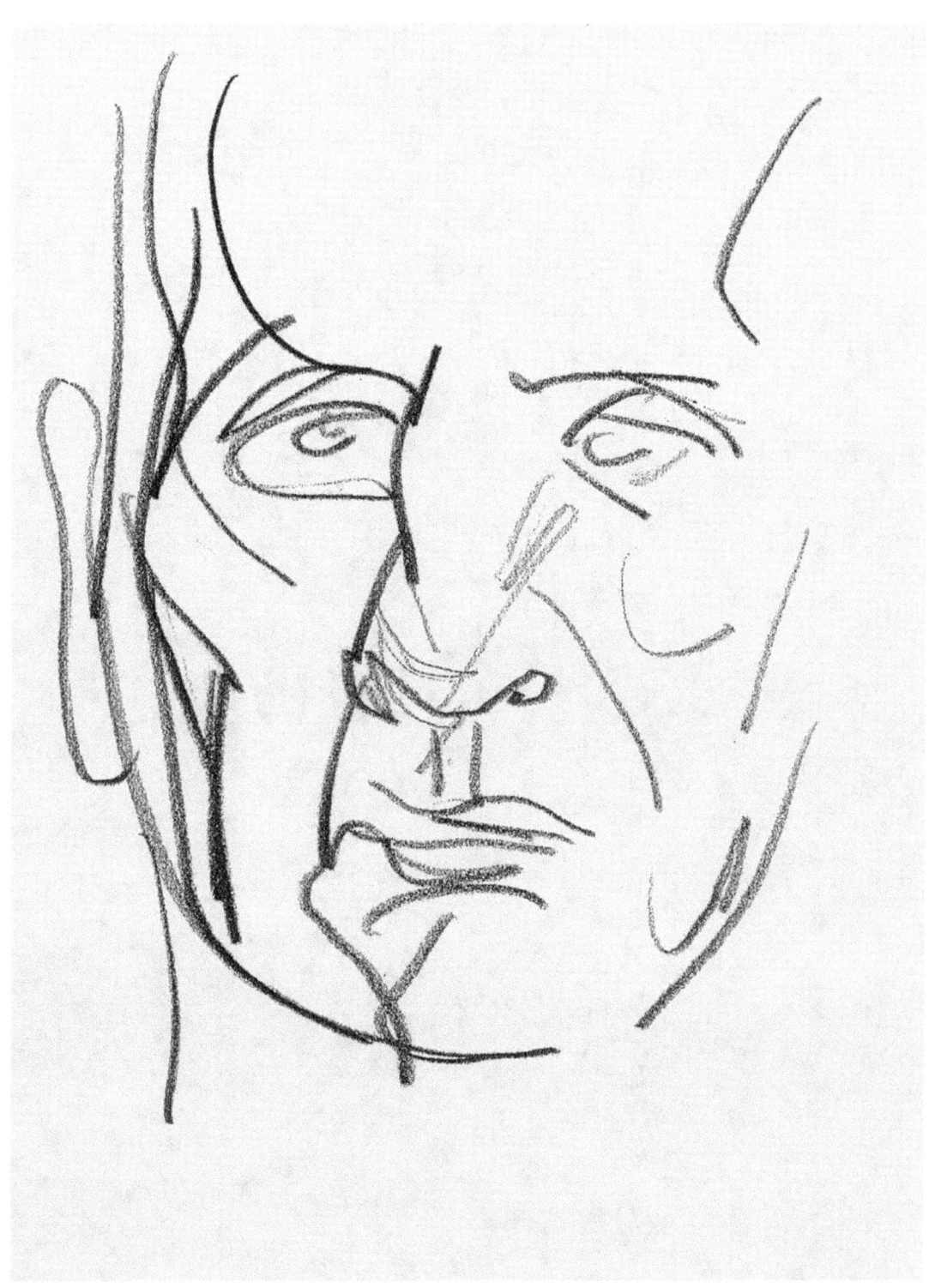

67    Face book, 2011, Pencil